Learn to Love:

A Couple's Guide to a Healthy Relationship

How to Cultivate Intimacy, Enhance Passion, Strengthen Commitment, and Improve Communication While Resolving Conflict With Your Partner

by Jaslin & Yusuf Varzideh

INFINITE
CREATIONS

Visit the author's website at www.infinitecreationsinc.com.

Contents

"I would like to thank you, Yusuf, for your extreme dedication to this book, to your wife (me), and to the world. We did it! We wrote the book! Woo-hoo!"

~ Jaslin

∞

"This book (and my wildest dreams) are possible because of you, Jaslin Varzideh, my wife, my love, my soulmate, my world."

~ Yusuf

Introduction

Learning to Love

> *"Intimate relationships bring us the most happiness in our lives but are the least mastered."*
>
> \- Tony Robbins

Why do so many romantic relationships end in breakups? In the US alone, between 2000 and 2020, 630,505 marriages ended.[1] How many people can you think of who are still together after many years and who passionately desire each other? Are they also intimate on a deep level, commit to each other totally, and want to be together for the rest of their lives? In our experience, it is much easier to find couples who are unsatisfied with their relationship and longing for more.

Suffice to say, there is room for improvement in this problem we are having! We need a solution for this worldwide relationship issue. Maybe you did, but we never learned a thing in grade school about how to have good relationships, how to communicate compassionately, or how to love.

When you consider your own love life, how often have you experienced unconditional love from your partner? When did you last feel passionate about your relationship? Do you trust your partner and feel accepted and safe with them? How can your relationship start to thrive? We'd like to help you answer these questions so you can enjoy a union that is alive and growing.

This interests us due to how much we learned and overcame together to create the beautiful partnership we have now. At this stage in our relationship, five years after meeting at a Tony Robbins event, we are living our dream life as digital nomads, traveling the world and working remotely from anywhere we choose. The best thing about our relationship is how close we are, how passionate we are, and how committed we are to each other. We have an incredible amount of love for one another, and we both consider ourselves to be the luckiest people on the planet because we have both found our soulmates in each other.

Our relationship is a fairy tale now because of what we did before and after we met. We got together after attending many workshops and seminars and reading hundreds of books on communication, relationships, and life. We both took a break from our relationships before meeting to better understand ourselves. As a result, once we met, we were better equipped to deal with the complexities of social relationships. Then we discovered so much about each other that we thought we knew each other better than ourselves. This proved to be a strong foundation on which to build.

However, it wasn't always sunshine and rainbows. We had our challenges. Sometimes we disagreed. Sometimes we argued. Sometimes we would even yell. We noticed past relationship pains were showing up in our present partnership. We both had unpleasant experiences of cheating and verbal abuse in previous relationships, so we didn't trust our partner out of fear of the past repeating itself. We broke up twice early on because of this. We clearly didn't understand each other. We needed to learn how to interact and be with each other without crossing boundaries, forcing wills, or people-pleasing. We needed to learn how to love. This was no simple task because of our upbringing, since no one taught us how to love the way we wished to be loved.

When we were kids, both sets of our parents fought *all* the time, and both marriages ended eventually. No offense to them, but neither one of us wanted to have the relationships our parents had, so throughout the years we asked for advice from other couples. Yet nobody in our vicinity gave us wisdom that worked for us.

Instead, we turned to each other. We asked each other a lot of questions, read a lot of books together, and visited a lot of seminars to improve our relationship. Diving deeper into our own internal worlds to learn what we wanted in our relationship and about each other proved to be a better strategy for learning how to have a healthy relationship.

One important concept we learned about that helped immensely was the feminine and masculine polarities. If we understood why people do what they do, we could communicate better. Things started clicking for us. This helped us bring out the best in each other, rather than the worst.

After a few years, we're so in love that we cannot stand seeing other people's relationships suffer anymore. As a result, we wrote this book to help others have a healthy relationship. Everything you're about to read, we did ourselves as a couple. We are grateful for every heartbreak and challenge we faced in the past because, without those experiences, we would not have been able to write this in the same way or with the same amount of passion. We hope the advice provided here brings you as much joy, love, and freedom as it has for us.

We knew we had found a winning formula when our friends started coming to us for relationship advice. Even older friends became curious about how they could have a more meaningful connection, like the one we share. This book applies to every person of any age because the principles are universal (even in same-sex relationships).

What we share in this book worked for us. It doesn't mean it will work for you, but it has supported our friends and family in their romantic endeavors. We believe if you apply your full effort to the principles and practices of this book, your relationship will have more passion, intimacy, commitment, and love. This book can also give you clarity on whether your relationship is where you want it to be and how you can take it to the next level.

A principle that appears often in this book is the concept of polarity. We believe in nonduality as a philosophy, which states there is only one infinite creator in existence and everything in the universe is part of it. For the purposes of this book, however, it is important to note that our environment clearly exhibits two polarities in the form of positive and negative, left and right, up and down, dark and light. Since relationships are a part of this environment, they must have two polar opposite sides as well: unhealthy relationships and healthy relationships.

We want to show you how to rebuild a healthy relationship even if you and your partner regularly argue and barely have sex, which is more indicative of an unhealthy relationship. What is a healthy relationship? We define it as a loving relationship where two people are intimate, passionate, committed, and communicate compassionately together. Even if you are in a not-so-awful relationship but it lacks passion or intimacy, we will show you how to rekindle the spark. This way, you can breathe new life into it.

Before starting our relationship, we almost gave up on pursuing romance. Thank God we didn't give up because being without love and other people can be harmful to our health. In Chapter 1, we'll look at why having a relationship is so worthwhile. We'll talk about the extensive research on the benefits of healthy relationships and the long-term effects of unhealthy ones.

In addition, if we desire healthy relationships, we must be conscious of our choices and what drives us (as well as our partner). What do you suppose happens if our thoughts determine our actions, and most of us are unaware and unconscious of our thoughts and actions? We get into unhealthy relationships. To address this issue, we must understand ourselves and our partners, which we show you how to do in Chapter 2.

Once you know and understand yourself and your partner better, we'll move on to Chapter 3, which is about understanding your relationship and what it needs to thrive. There are certain ingredients that make your relationship a soulmate union. Without these ingredients, it can feel more like being in prison or living with a roommate.

In Chapter 4, we tell you the truth about where your relationship stands right now. Most people pick up this book wanting to improve their love lives. If something isn't growing, it's dying. Knowing this, people naturally want to grow, expand, and move forward in their relationships and in all parts of their lives. To progress and have more in our relationships, we first have to know where we are and then decide to move to the next level. We will explain this further in Chapter 4.

In Chapters 5, 6, and 7, we cover the different approaches that will move you into a more passionate, intimate, and committed relationship. We will show you how to revive your existing romantic partnership so it can flourish. Whether you're on the brink of breaking up because the spark has gone, or if you're full of spark but lacking depth, we will show you how to move to the next level. This way, love blossoms and your relationship thrives.

In Chapter 8, we cover the framework we use to avoid fights and how to communicate in a way that brings more understanding, harmony, and unity. Humans disagree sometimes, but what you do and how you act when you disagree can make all the difference. What if there is a way for you to agree that supports you both? That's what you'll discover in Chapter 8.

Finally, in Chapter 9, we talk about how to make your revived union last for the long run so you can maintain this new level of intimacy, passion, and commitment through tough times.

Throughout this book, we did our best to include conscious inclusive language so that every person and their relationships can get something from it without concern. Nevertheless, please understand that we may use traditional language from time to time because we are in a heterosexual relationship, but we also did our best throughout the book to make it gender-neutral and used specific context to make this book as bias-free as humanly possible.

You will notice we use words like female, male, feminine, and masculine energies within the book. While talking about female and male, please understand we mean the assigned gender role given to someone at birth, which includes certain common characteristics such as specific hormones in the body that can affect how a person thinks and feels. It is also important to understand that every relationship has one partner who is more masculine and one partner who is more feminine. No matter the energy that you feel more connected to, there are feminine and masculine energies within any relationship, including same-sex relationships.

With all that said, we do use "she/her/hers" and "he/him/his" pronouns in the examples. However, we did our best to include "they/them/their" pronouns throughout the text so that every couple, no matter the core essence or assigned gender at birth, can feel included and so couples can read this book together. We are not experts on the constant evolution of language, but we did our best to be intentional and respectful of everyone to have the best reading experience possible.

We should also note that we are a happily married couple, so we can only speak from experience about how we view relationships and marriage. Some see us as a 'traditional' relationship, and to others, it is everything but traditional (since we travel full time and haven't had a permanent home in 3+ years). Regardless, it is our way of life, and we speak from the experience and research we have gathered over the years. You may have a different point of view, yet you can still gain plenty of important information from this book. Whether or not you are married, this book can help you thrive in romantic relationships. If you disagree with a particular point, simply ignore it and move on.

For a relationship with two or more partners, while this book's principles can still work for you, we intend it for couples choosing monogamy. We designed this book for relationships involving two people who want to keep it that way. However, you can apply most of these principles to all of your romantic partnerships.

Your newfound union will require some effort at first. As Newton's First Law of Motion tells us, a body remains at rest or in motion unless acted upon by an outside force.[2] Your relationship is where it is now either because you haven't tried to change it or because it's headed in the wrong direction as a result of past behavior. If you don't want negative outside factors to change the course of your relationship, you must take action and move it in the direction you want. This book will give you that new direction. There is always hope, no matter the road you are already on.

If you are willing to move in that new direction, then buckle up for the most worthwhile ride of your life—the journey of love. Are you ready for a more healthy relationship? Follow us to Chapter 1.

Chapter 1

Why Invest in a Relationship?

∞

We need people. We cannot exist without each other. Without human contact, a baby will die. No company can function on its own, or it will fail. We usually only live in isolation as a punishment (for example, in prison for inappropriate behavior) or because of an accident (like being stranded on an island). Long periods of separation from others can drive us wild, as you may have heard in stories.

Relationships are important for our mental and emotional health. They are also necessary to our survival because, without other people, our species would disappear. We are social animals; men and women communicate and form strong bonds through relationships. This means that the quality of our relationships affects how happy we feel. Our ability to form and maintain relationships allows us to form complex social networks.

Several academic disciplines have studied how important relationships are:

- **Sociologists** study interpersonal relationships within and between communities.
- **Anthropologists** research how people in various communities form connections and interact with one another.
- **Psychologists** investigate how relationship issues can lead to conflict, mental illness, and unhappiness.

Here's the thing: As individuals, we can freely think and act. As adults, we can meet our basic needs of food, shelter, and water alone. We can also provide our own safety and security, eliminating the need for relationships. People have survived alone in the woods, right? The question then becomes, "Why do humans place such a high value on healthy relationships if people have survived alone?"

Science shows that we are less independent than we may believe. To understand the role that relationships play in human behavior, let's examine Abraham Maslow's hierarchy of needs.[3] This ranking sums up the key requirements that people need to be stable and happy. It shows the quality of human life, and when it is low, it causes dissatisfaction, depression, and, in extreme cases, death. These requirements form the order in the shape of a pyramid. Basic needs like food, water, and shelter are at the bottom, and self-actualization is at the top. Love and belonging are at the center.

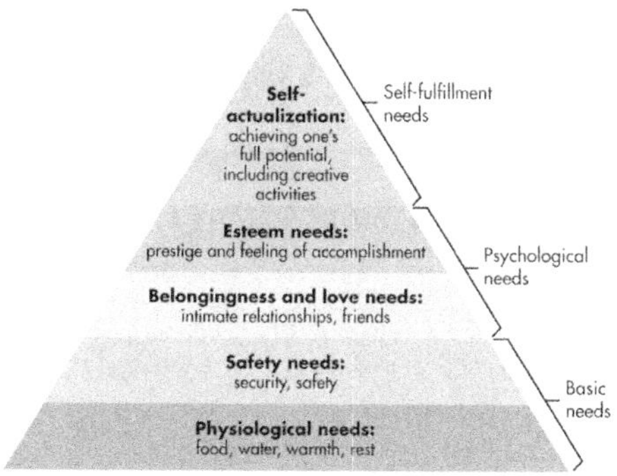

Figure 1: Abraham Maslow's hierarchy of needs[4]

Relationships satisfy this psychological need for love and belonging. This means that the love and belonging that relationships provide are necessary for our happiness. It allows us to understand humans as a species with individual will and a group that needs close relationships with others to be stable and happy.

What makes a healthy relationship good for us? What do you picture when thinking of people in "healthy relationships"? Do you picture people smiling, talking, and laughing? Even thinking about it makes us happy. What is the source of these emotions we experience when we socialize? Oxytocin. People's brains release this love drug when they snuggle, have sex, or bond socially.[5]

Oxytocin helps us live longer, healthier lives by defending the brain from stress. Stress kills. People say things like "you're going to give me a heart attack," because stress can cause a heart attack. An academic review of oxytocin reports that the brain regulates the release of stress hormones, and oxytocin protects brain neurons from the damage of stress.[6] Stress reduction can lead to a happier, healthier, and longer life. If oxytocin protects our brain from stress, then it makes sense that more oxytocin can lead us to a happier, healthier, and longer life, too.

What happens if oxytocin levels are low? "Low oxytocin levels have been linked to symptoms of depression," according to Harvard Health.[7] When oxytocin levels are low, there is nothing to protect your brain from stress, increasing your risk of depression. This appears to be a lose-lose situation. It's no surprise that "married persons have the lowest suicide rates."[8]

The Benefits of Being in a Healthy Relationship

A healthy relationship is important because it is a basic human need. Research shows that a healthy relationship can improve your health. Building and maintaining a healthy relationship takes effort, but the resulting benefits are more than worth it.

Many people believe relationships are all about the spark. However, they're overlooking the deeper advantages of having someone who knows you, accepts you, makes you laugh, and always has your back when you need help.

More Happiness, Less Regret

Recall the last time you got into a heated argument. Consider how angry you were when you transformed from Bruce Banner to the Hulk. Did you notice your heart rate, the sweat on your palms, or the veins popping in your neck and head? Were you able to unwind and fall asleep right away? Our guess is no, because arguments cause anger, which affects our sympathetic nervous system responsible for our fight-or-flight response. Our body doesn't know the difference between an argument and getting attacked by a bear, so it reacts in the same way. This shows that relationships affect physical health.

Let's push the point even further by discussing what happens when you die (what a way to start a paragraph, huh?). In a study on the top ten regrets of the dying, relationship issues accounted for half of the major regrets.[9] People said things like, "I should have said 'I love you' a lot more," and "I worked too much and never made time for my family." If we want to avoid regrets at the end of our lives, we must not wait until we're close to death to prioritize relationships over work, status, and other things that don't contribute as much to our ultimate happiness.

If happiness is your goal, read the findings of the Harvard Second Generation Study, a 75-year study on happiness .[10] From 1939 to 2014, Harvard researchers studied 456 people from Boston's lower-income neighborhoods, and 268 people from Harvard's classes of 1939–1944. They have gathered the findings after decades of following and testing these groups. "The clearest message that we get from this 75-year study is this: Good relationships keep us happier and healthier," said Robert Waldinger in his TED Talk, What Makes a Good Life.[11] So, if you want to be healthy and happy, keep reading.

Better Mental Health

Healthy relationships can improve our mental health, but toxic relationships can do the opposite. Do you remember a time when you were feeling low but had no one to talk to or confide in? It's a very lonely feeling. Maintaining healthy relationships can provide you with the support you need to get through challenging times.

In a review of research on relationships and mental health, researchers found that "improving relationships improves mental health."[12] Your partner can help you get through tough times and provide stability in your life. Studies show that people in happy relationships have fewer depressive symptoms than those who are single, divorced, separated, widowed, or in troubled relationsh ips.[13]

If you are in a happy relationship, you can rely on your partner to support you through good and bad times. They'll be your biggest supporter and your shoulder to cry on. The weight of the world is lighter when we have someone else helping to carry it.

Better Physical Health

We could all use encouragement and a little nudge to stick to healthy habits, like eating well and exercising. It's easier to work toward your goals when you have a partner who believes in you and is rooting for you to succeed. When you step on the scale, having someone there to push away the fourth bag of Cheetos can mean the difference between frowning and smiling. There is also the desire to look good for your significant other, which often makes you want to be more active and eat better.

According to the study, "Better Together: The Impact of Exercising with a Romantic Partner," exercising with a romantic partner makes you more successful at the activity.[14] If you struggle to stick to a workout routine or get in shape, exercising with a loved one can help.

The same study also found, "on days when people exercised with their romantic partner, they experienced higher positive affect during exercise, higher daily positive affect, and were more satisfied with their relationship compared to days when they exercised alone."[15] So, if you want to feel more positive and satisfied with your relationship, try lifting weights together, taking a walk, or a fitness class.

Better Health = Longer Life

One of the many benefits that stands out is what it can do for our health and lifespan. According to this survey from the University of Warwick on how marriage affects physical and psychological health, "married people live longer and are healthier."[16] It's supported by a meta-analysis looking at over 250,000 older adults, which found that divorced, never-married, or widowed people have higher mortality risks than those who are married.[17]

Scientists looked at data from 148 research studies involving 308,849 participants. They found a 50% greater likelihood of survival for participants with stronger social relationships in a 2010 study in the journal PLOS Medicine. They discovered that those with the strongest social relationships had a 50% better chance of being alive at the end of a research period than those with no such ties.[18]

Research has shown that people in unhealthy relationships can have a weakened immune system.[19] This means unhealthy relationships can expose you to infectious diseases and cancer, resulting in poor health.

What happens if a toxic relationship lasts? What if arguments went on daily? Do you believe it will affect how long you live? You bet! According to a meta-analysis, studies show an increased risk of death among people with an unhealthy social relationship.[20]

Is it possible that being single and having a great social life are enough to keep us alive for longer? Not quite. "It's not only being married that promotes health," BYU psychologist and professor, Julianne Holt-Lunstad, said in an article.[21] "What's truly the most protective of health is having a happy marriage." She led another study which found that high marriage quality was linked to lower blood pressure, less stress, less sadness, and higher life satisfaction.[22] This proves that a pleasant, healthy relationship with your partner is health-protective.

Higher Self-Esteem

When someone loves you, they see things in you that you may not have noticed about yourself. Their positive perception of you can boost your self-esteem and self-confidence. How do you suppose that carries over to your career, business, or social life? It has a direct impact, especially when your partner reminds you of the potential within you on days when you feel low or insecure.

It reminded us of the folklore of a woman who believed in a frog and harnessed his greatness to turn him into a prince. The owner of Acquisition.com, Alex Hormozi, is a prime example of this. At 26, he was sleeping on a gym floor every night. Then he met his wife, Leila, and six years later, the couple's business was turning over more than $85 million per year. You can accomplish amazing things when you have a partner who believes in you.

Personal Growth

A good relationship can help you become a better person. You learn to talk with each other better, find the middle ground, and be more understanding. You also learn about yourself, such as what brings you joy and what stresses you out.

Relationships force us to improve because they give us feedback on things we wouldn't notice without someone else's reflection. Have you ever told jokes you thought were hilarious, only to discover later that your partner found them rude or insensitive? You could have continued telling these jokes, potentially hurting others' feelings. Personal development is less likely without the help of someone close by to keep us in check.

Better Sleep

Imagine cuddling under a blanket with your loved one. Doesn't it feel warmer and safer, which makes it easier to sleep? In addition, sleeping beside a partner reduces stress levels and improves sleep quality, according to a study from the University of Pittsburgh.[23]

More Positive Emotions and Overall Satisfaction

When we share emotions, they increase. Doing something that feels good feels even better when we have someone to share it with. Why do most people go to the movies or eat out with someone, rather than alone? Sharing experiences increases our positive emotions.

Most people think they want 'things' in life, but is that ever the final goal? What people want are the feelings that come from those "things." For example, if you want a raise, it's because more money will bring you more security, abundance, and freedom. So, since we are all after feelings, guess what gives us more positive emotions? Relationships! According to a study from the University of Hawaii, positive emotion is associated with relationship satisfaction.[24]

Service to Others

Have we persuaded you that healthy relationships are a good thing? They improve your health, help you live longer, make you happier, and prevent you from dying with regret and loneliness? If you're still not convinced, that's fine; perhaps you've had little luck with your partner. While you are in your current circumstances and environment, it's tough to see beyond them, but that's why you're reading this book—because you're looking for solutions. And we can provide them.

Now that you know relationships are important, we have one decision to make. We want to offer you a choice regarding whom you are going to serve more in this lifetime: yourself, or your partner and the relationship. In The Law of One, they call these options Service to Self (putting yourself before others) and Service to Others (putting others before yourself).[25] Since everything ultimately serves the self, the path of Service To Others serves the self by serving others. This path will put others at the expense of the self. The path of Service To Self serves the self at the expense of others because it puts self before anything and anyone else most of the time.

Every moment, we are making that choice, even if we are unaware of it. So, it's time to make that choice consciously. From here on out, decide whose needs and desires you want to prioritize most in each moment—yours or your partner's. Service to Others is a path of love, unity, harmony, and forgiveness. Service to Self is the path of fear, separation, chaos, control, and hatred.

When you choose Service to Others, you are deciding you will put someone else before yourself. We don't mean as a martyr would, because you still have to survive. However, most of the time, if you choose to serve others, you choose unity over separation, love over fear, and forgiveness over hate. The path of Service to Self puts yourself first at the expense of others, creating dominance, control, competition, and separation. This does not lead to a healthy relationship.

The path of Service to Others leads to a healthy relationship because you are serving your partner. This is the path where you make your relationship a priority and care enough about your relationship to make it work. When conflict begins, you serve your relationship by forgiving, loving, devoting yourself to them, and making it work by using the principles and journal prompts in this book.

Which path will you choose?

If you are still reading, we assume you have chosen the path of Service to Others, which is the path of service to your partner. Now that you have made the choice, the rest of this book is a matter of staying committed to your chosen path, a.k.a. service to your partner and your relationship. Let's move on to the next steps.

We'll start by helping you understand yourself first and then your partner. If you're wondering why you should start with yourself, it's because relationships are all about how you relate to and interact with others. If you don't understand yourself, how can you expect others to understand you? Check out Chapter 2 if you're serious about getting to know yourself and your partner better. We will teach you a process for doing just that.

Journal Prompts

- What are some of the benefits of being in a healthy relationship?
- What choice did you make - service to self or service to others?
- How are you going to continue making this

choice on a daily basis?What is a "healthy relationship" to you?

Chapter 2

The Three Keys to Better Understanding Yourself and Your Partner

∞

There are three keys to a healthy relationship with your partner. Let's look at these, then dive into practical ways of applying them.

Key 1: Create a Healthy Relationship With Yourself

Since our outer world reflects our inner world, we must know ourselves before we can know others. Without knowing who you are, how will you ever be able to understand someone else, much less fully accept and love them?

To have a healthy relationship with yourself, you must first know yourself, then accept yourself, and finally love yourself. You can achieve this through self-awareness. Some find meditation and other esoteric methods helpful. However, for the more practically minded, we will show you how to reach an understanding of yourself through specific questions.

Key 2: Know Your Partner as Well as Yourself

We need to let go of what we believe we know about our partner and understand them beyond just their favorite foods and TV shows. Couples often invest more time and effort into learning about their partners in the early stages of a relationship. Then years pass and the "honeymoon phase" is over, life goes on, and that sense of wonder at being with someone new ends. Once the learning stops because of the needs of kids, work, and business, things can become stagnant. However, to bring your relationship out of the depths of boredom and/or misery, it's time to bring back the same curiosity that gave it life in the beginning. As Tony Robbins wrote, "If you do what you did in the beginning of the relationship, there won't be an end."[26]

Key 3: Bring This Knowledge Together

The third key to creating a healthy relationship is bringing your understanding of yourself and that of your partner together and creating a vision of your ultimate relationship. This requires you both to understand yourselves and each other, then join forces in harmony to co-create what you envision together.

Understanding Your Needs

Let's start with the most fundamental aspect of every human: our needs. We're not just talking about Maslow's hierarchy of needs, which includes food, water, and shelter. We all have these needs, which makes us all similar from this perspective. We are going to dive deeper into the needs that make us all unique.

The Six Human Needs

Have you ever wondered what motivates you to take action? All our actions come from one of two basic motivations: the desire to avoid pain or gain pleasure. Consider this: We drink coffee to enjoy the pleasure of feeling awake or to avoid the agony of sleeping in and losing our jobs.

Different things give us pleasure and help us avoid pain in different ways. What motivates us to seek pleasure or avoid pain are the six human needs as described by Tony Robbins:[27]

- **Certainty**: Knowing that we can avoid pain and

gain pleasure. We require being sure about what is going to happen next and feeling comfortable enough to survive.

- **Uncertainty/Variety**: We also need to change, new stimuli, and the unknown. Any change can meet this need, such as a change in food, environment, and people.

- **Significance**: The need to feel unique, important, special, or needed. We can meet this need by garnering attention, accolades, awards, and acknowledgment. We meet this need by being the biggest or best, or by making other people smaller or less than us.

- **Love/Connection**: Closeness or union with someone or something, such as a family member, friend, nature, God, the universe, or even ourselves. We can feel a connection toward someone physically (such as a hug or a punch), or emotionally (such as love or hate).

- **Growth**: The need to expand capacity, capability, or understanding. Growth could mean a new skill, learning anything, or even improving daily. Everything in this universe must grow or it withers, because stagnation is not a permanent state.

- **Contribution**: The need to give, support, help, serve, etc. We can contribute to one person, to a family, to a community, or to the world at large. Without contribution, our species would not survive; we must give to children for them to grow when they cannot give to themselves, or they would die.

We all have the same core needs but different orders of importance to them. So, how do these needs "drive" us to act? Our actions are determined by our needs and the order of importance we place on each.

Let's use a car, for example, and how two people may get that car to meet different needs. Person A says, "I want a car so I can travel and go to bookstores." This would show their primary human needs are uncertainty/variety and growth. Person B says, "I want a cool car that goes faster than all my friends' cars and that gets me home after work." This could show their top two human needs are certainty and significance. We each have distinct orders of priority. The order in which someone places their needs will determine how they act and the decisions they make throughout their lives.

It is important to note that, although we may guess someone else's needs, it is important to let them decide their own top needs and not second-guess them. Let each person choose their own top needs for themselves—including your partner.

Having one need rank higher than another is not right or wrong, but how we treat others while meeting those needs determines our character. For example, two people can have the top need of significance yet meet it in different ways: one person builds the biggest business they can by serving their clients well, and another might bring down other people's businesses that are similar to theirs. How we meet our needs, whether self-serving or in service to others, will determine our character even more than how we prioritize those needs.

Determining Your Needs

How do you determine your top needs? This is where self-inquiry comes into play. Ask yourself questions. One of the key questions here is: "What is life about?" This question is so revealing of what drives you as a human. Try it for yourself right now.

Let's imagine you say something like, "Life is about getting to the next level." Which need does that refer to? Growth because "getting to the next level" means growing, progressing, or "leveling up." If you said something like, "Life is about giving back," that means you need contribution. The phrase "Life is about family" would show you need love/connection. Go with the first answer you give, not what you think you should say. If you're honest with yourself, you can learn who you are at your core and not what you think others expect of you.

Once you have identified your primary human need, ask yourself the next question: "After [answer from above], what else is life about?" The second answer will give you insight into the next need on your list. Keep answering this question until you can't think of more answers. Now you have your list in order from most to least important. Your first answer is normally your top need and then every answer after that follows in order of importance. Your needs can change depending on your mood, so do this a few times to notice the pattern. When you get a consistent response, that is your order of needs.

Other Ways To Find Your Top Needs

Another way to find your top needs is by asking the people closest to you what they think *your* life is about. Ask them, "If I asked you what my life is all about, what would you say?" Let them answer without steering them toward a specific outcome. Sometimes, the people in our lives have better insight than us because they see us from a different perspective and give us an outside reference on what we are really like when we are lost in our own world.

Also, look at your actions and see where you often give up one need for another. The question for this is, "What do I often sacrifice to meet this need?" Do you sacrifice comfort (certainty) to be the best of the best at something (significance)? Have you frequently given up spending time with friends or family (connection) to read more or learn a new skill (growth)? Do you often give up fun (variety) to take care of someone in your life (contribution)? Do you give up meeting with friends (a.k.a. connection) to meet your need to stay home and watch TV (a.k.a. certainty) often?

These are key insights into what's driving you to act. There's nothing wrong with any of your answers; one need is just more important to you than the other. No matter what, it's important to be honest with yourself, or else you won't come to true understanding.

How Do You Meet Your Needs?

We all meet our needs in different ways because we're all different. For instance, Bob meets his need for connection by spending time with nature and meditating in the morning. Sally meets her need for connection by being surrounded by lots of people. John meets his need for connection by spending time with his wife and dog. They each meet the same need, but in unique ways.

Journal Prompts

- What are your top two human needs?
- How do you meet your top two human needs?
- What are your partner's top two human needs?
- How does your partner meet their top two human needs?

Understanding Your Values

Next, we will dive into another part of ourselves that makes us unique: our values. These are things we consider valuable and most important to us. What one person finds meaningful, another person might find meaningless. As a couple, you can identify similarities or differences in values to understand each other better. It is much easier for your partner to know what you value if you both know what that is.

For example, if one person values peace and another values control above all else, their interactions with loved ones and the world at large will be different. One might concede to keep the peace while the other fights for control. Different values make for a completely unique way of going about life. Our values create unique thoughts, perspectives, and actions.

Understanding values also helps us build stronger bonds because you'll know them at a deeper level than just their material desires. Values influence what a person cares about or pays attention to, and knowing this allows you to know them more intimately.

By understanding your partner's core values, you can understand how they meet their needs, which leads to a better understanding of them as a person. In the example above, both individuals are looking to meet their need for certainty through peace or control—the same human need, but two different ways of meeting it. One person wants to keep the peace so they might remain calm in their dealings with others; the other acts in search of control, which isn't very peaceful. We humans are complex beings!

Identifying Your Values

Since there are different values, let's discuss two types: mean values and end values. Mean values are a means to an end. For example, if you ask someone what is most important to them, they might say family, career, or even something more tangible, like their house or their car. These are the means. We take this a step further by asking, "Why?" Why is your family, the house, or the car important to you?

Once we can boil it down to a feeling, we have landed on the end value. We do this because we don't want things, people, places, or experiences in life. We want the feelings they give us. We want the feelings that our job, family, house, or car gives us like freedom, love, abundance, joy, etc.

If we look at the example above, we can see how we can phrase this question: "What would _____ (family, house, car, etc.) provide for you?" Or: "What is the feeling that X gives me?" The house is a means of freedom, love, joy, peace, etc. Someone might say their car makes them feel secure. Another person might say it provides adventure for them. Now we know their values, and perhaps their needs, all at the same time. Do this for every area of your own life to discover what's most important to you, then repeat for your partner.

Journal Prompts

- What is most important to you in life?
- What are the feelings those [things, people or places] give you?
- What feeling is *most* important for you to feel in life?
- What are your top five values in order of impor-

tance?

- What are your partner's top five values in order of importance?
- How can you help your partner feel these values?
- How can your partner help you to feel these values?

Understanding Your Rules

The next step is to identify your rules. These are ways in which you meet your needs and values. Rules are important because we seldom know explicitly that we have specific criteria for things. People walk around getting offended and hurt because they don't realize their rules are being violated. If we can notice how to meet certain needs and values, we can have fewer arguments and thus more connection and understanding.

It's important to know this because you and your partner might both desire a specific feeling, such as fun, but you might meet it in different ways. For instance, you might enjoy playing video games for fun, while your partner might prefer skydiving. The feeling is the same, but you fulfill it in different ways based on your rules, which you might be unaware of. This is useful information for considering dates, things to do together, and even chores around the house. What would happen if you have a need for certainty (as security) and your rule for meeting that need is you lock the car even if you are close by? Yet, your partner leaves it open since they don't know your rule? You might get upset unless you clarify this rule, create boundaries, and thus acknowledge needs or values.

If you don't know your partner's rules and they don't know yours, this can create conflict. We have rules for everything, yet they often go unnoticed or unexpressed. However, if you are already aware of your own needs, values, and rules, it will be much easier to understand theirs and express yours to them when needed.

Identifying Your Rules

How do you discover your rules? Fill in the blanks: "I feel [insert value] when I _____." For example, "I feel accomplished when I finish all my tasks on time." So, if your partner interrupts you and you get upset, now you will understand WHY you get upset, and so will they. This helps your partner (and other people) understand you better and gives them a chance to help you feel accomplished (or meet your other needs or values).

Often, when someone knows or believes that someone else intentionally violated their rules, you'll hear phrases like "You disrespected me" or "You did that on purpose!"

The way we can avoid violating someone's rules is by being aware of them—which we are doing here—and then sharing them with your partner so they can be in your corner to help you.

For example, "What has to happen for me to feel free? After work, I need time to go exploring in the woods by myself for at least an hour." When that time comes, your partner will know, and they can give you an hour to meet the level of freedom you require.

You can share this list of rules with your partner and agree together. If there are non-negotiable rules for you, discuss them together. Go through the lists you created earlier for your values and write your rules for each. Notice what comes up. Write your answers to see how you could meet these values. When done, add, delete, or change your rules for meeting your values in a way that fits who you wish to be in your life and your relationships.

Journal Prompts

- What are your rules for each of your five values?
- What are your partner's rules for each of their five values?
- How can your partner support you in meeting your rules?

- How can you support your partner in meeting their rules?

Understanding Your Goals

Humans have a need for growth; an innate urge to want more from life. Goal-setting is essential to moving forward. Whether or not you're the ambitious type, you have goals, even if you're not aware of them. Even simple things like getting enough food or water are goals.

Our goals can help us have what we want in life with our partner. When you understand your own goals, you can share them with your partner and the two of you can talk about what support you need to achieve them. When your partner knows what you want because you know what you want, they can join your team (so to speak) in helping you achieve this. If you don't know your own goals, how can your partner make it easier for you to achieve them?

This next step is about realizing your goals so you can share them with your partner and learn about their goals as well. As Robin Jones Gunn once said, "If you want to go fast, go alone. If you want to go far, go together."[28]

The question for understanding your goals is: "What do I want in/for my life?" You can ask this question for every area of life, including relationships, health, and business.

Working Toward Your Goals

Once you have identified your goals, you can break them down into smaller goals and start creating timelines and action steps. For instance, if your goal is to save $30,000 to buy a house, sharing this with your partner is vital in making sure you don't argue about spending money. If you'd like to save $30,000 by the end of the year, you could set a timeline for specific milestones. You could set a goal of $7,500 in three months, $15,000 in six months, and $30,000 by the end of the year. Do this for every area of your life: health, business and career, finances, family, relationships, social, home and living, spirituality, and fun/recreation.

Once you've established your goals and broken them down, you can ask: "How can my partner support me in this goal?" Maybe if your partner spent less, you would reach your goal of saving $30,000 more quickly. Maybe your partner can contribute to saving that amount. Every goal is easier if more than one person contributes to it. Just ask!

Working Together

This is about coming up with goals together for your life and relationship. Once you have listed your goals and your partner's goals, share them with each other to check for any overlap. From there, create a goals list for your relationship and life together. This will be your relationship vision, which is the life you're headed towards together. Having no vision or direction is like shooting darts in the dark. Creating a vision together is the first step toward a new direction.

The last part of this section involves creating a vision board together of your life as a couple, because a picture is worth a thousand words. Create a shared vision statement and an affirmation board that represents the highest ideals of your relationship. This shared vision statement and affirmation board will represent you as a couple and what you'd like to present together to the world.

Journal Prompts

- What are your long-term goals?
- What are your short-term goals?
- How can your partner support you with your goals?
- What are your partner's long-term goals?
- What are your partner's short-term goals?
- How can you support your partner's goals?

- What's your relationship's vision statement?
- Create a vision board for both of your goals together. Share your vision board together! (Use any template you find online, or just put photos on a board, and try not to overthink it!)

Putting it All Together

Now that you understand yourself and your partner, what do you do with all that information? You can use it to get what you want, help them get what they want, and ease many misunderstandings and conflicts that occur from not knowing what drives each other.

Be careful not to misuse this information. Don't use it as a way of manipulating them. However, since you have already made the choice to be of service to your partner and the relationship, you won't be that person. Use this knowledge to support your partner and your relationship.

Whatever your partner is doing, you now know what is driving them to act. You also know how they like to meet those needs and values (a.k.a. rules), so everything becomes easier. Behind the certain states we want are emotions, and in helping your partner feel those emotions, you get a teammate, not a cellmate. This makes for a healthier relationship.

Instead of getting upset that your partner isn't doing what you want them to, you now understand they have different motivations than you. Knowing they might want more security while you want more fun is valuable information. Imagine how much smoother life could be when people knew what they needed and wanted.

Now that you understand each other better, it's time to bring more love into your relationship. As easy as that sounds, there's a lot more to it, because love is more than one feeling. It comprises several feelings, which we call ingredients. In the following chapter, we'll discuss those three ingredients of love and how to incorporate more of each into your relationship so that it thrives and you can learn to love in more ways than one.

Chapter 3

The Three Ingredients of a Healthy Relationship

∞

What is the single most important aspect of a healthy relationship? Love. If we had to boil down the essence of love to its basic ingredients, what would they be? Consider what happens when you fall in love. You first notice the other person and like them. Then the liking develops into a strong desire for them. That desire turns into a yearning to keep them around for a longer time. That longer time shows up as a series of increasingly permanent steps. These may look like a drawer designated just for them, then a promise ring, then a puppy, then a diamond on the finger, and someday kids. Your series of events may be different, but you get the picture.

As a result, three key parts make up the fullness of love:

- Affection/Intimacy
- Passion
- Commitment

Love = Affection + Passion + Commitment

People in a relationship perceive love differently, depending on how much of these three "ingredients" they share.

For centuries, humans have tried to define love in poems, books, and dictionaries. Search online for "love," and you'll see several definitions pop up:

Love definition, according to The Britannica Dictionary:

1. a feeling of strong or constant affection for a person
2. attraction that includes sexual desire: the strong affection felt by people who have a romantic relationship[1]

Within these definitions, we see two ingredients out of three: affection and passion (sexual desire). We can see how most romantic relationships contain both passion and affection. However, without commitment, the affection and passion would not endure, and most relationships would not last beyond a one-night stand.

Most romantic relationships have stages. They progress based on how much love is shared, and we have names for each stage, such as a crush, dating, engagement, and marriage. Above all, the amount of commitment between the two parties moves the relationship from a crush to a long-term partnership. In the following section, we discuss how these three ingredients (or the lack of them) affect your relationship and how to enhance them for a love story worth telling. Which ingredient could you use more of to spice up your relationship?

Ingredient #1: Affection/Intimacy

Affection definition, according to The Britannica Dictionary: "a feeling of liking and caring for someone or something."[30]

Intimacy definition, according to The Britannica Dictionary: "an intimate quality or state: such as emotional warmth and closeness."[31]

Throughout this book, for simplicity's sake, we'll use the terms "affection" and "intimacy" interchangeably.

Affection is the substance that makes your connection sweet. Affection is like honey in a relationship. Consider the difference between a plain cup of tea and a cup of tea with honey. Which lingers longer on your taste buds and is more popular? Of course, the one with honey.

Affection generally starts with shared interests or commonalities. Think about someone you met in your class at some point. What bonded you? Maybe you shared an interest in something the teacher said, or you shared another class together, or you had the same backpack. They define affection as "a feeling of liking and caring for someone," and what gets someone to like you? When you are like them. We like people who are like us. How intimacy is defined shows us it's about having a close personal relationship with somebody, which can only happen when they know, like, and trust you (which you will learn in Chapter 5.)

Have you ever felt comfortable with someone but you're not attracted to them? That's affection alone. You give them loads of support, you love communicating with them, but there is no "spark," so you friend-zone them. Affection alone is not enough for love; if you stay as friends only, love will never flourish. That's why you need passion for the relationship to move from friendship to something more.

Ingredient #2: Passion

Passion definition, according to The Britannica Dictionary: "a strong sexual or romantic feeling for someone."[32]

Sexual desire (a.k.a. passion) is necessary for a healthy relationship because it drives the need for more of your loved one. There is no sensuality or sexuality between people without desire, so passion is a necessary ingredient for a love connection. Passion creates the 'spice' of your relationship. Have you ever noticed how the country of India is famed for its spicy cuisine and Kama Sutra books? There might be a connection. Spices such as ginger add a 'kick' to our foods, and "It's an aphrodisiac by increasing sperm percent, viability, motility, and serum total testosterones."[33] The chemical components of passion in our brains have a similar effect.

You can have a relationship without this ingredient, but it would be like two roommates living together, or worse, two cellmates forced to be together because of family or finances. Consider passion to be your relationship's aphrodisiac, stimulating sexual desire. Without this, there's no desire for two people to be lovers, and the relationship will either become one-sided or slowly die off.

Most of the time, passion has a physical component to it, such as that moment when someone catches your attention in a room full of people, but passion isn't only sudden, it can also be created. The intensity of your desire for something can raise your passion level. You can create passion in a single phrase, such as "I want you." Smelling someone's pheromones can raise your passion meter. Someone else can also increase your desire for them by expressing their interest in you. There are countless ways you can spark desire, even after years of being together.

This is where the well-known term "the spark" comes from. Mutual desire between two people creates that spark. You sense it, they sense it, and sparks fly. Pheromones, along with the reactions in our brains, release a group of hormones and neurotransmitters (including dopamine and oxytocin).[34] This creates a tremendous wave of passion that characterizes the "spark" moment we see in the movies.

You can also have a relationship based on passion alone, although it is likely to be lust-filled but unfulfilling or short-lived. If there are no other ingredients, it will leave nothing behind. A "booty call" is an example of a relationship that has more passion than anything else. This is someone you hook up with just for the night and for nothing more than sex. There's no chatting about each other's innermost secrets or staying over for breakfast with your parents the next day. Just rough and tumble between the sheets, then off to your own lives.

The problem with passion is that, being an emotion, it comes and goes. Have you ever had such a powerful urge for a favorite food that you couldn't stop thinking about it? What if you ate an enormous platter of it? Do you still desire it as much? Probably not. The tremendous desire and passion are no longer there. So, passion alone will not sustain a relationship until you include another ingredient—commitment.

Ingredient #3: Commitment

Commitment definition, according to The Britannica Dictionary: "a promise to be loyal to someone or somet hing."[35]

If commitment were an ingredient in a recipe, it would be salt. It enriches the dish and pulls everything together. Although salt is the most basic flavor, it enhances any food we add it to, and the longer it sits, the better it tastes. Salt also makes food last longer because it is a preservative. In the world of relationships, commitment helps a fling survive longer than a one-night stand and may even turn it into a happily ever after. The level of commitment between lovers determines whether they have a short-term infatuation or a lifelong love story.

Commitment determines the relationship's pace. Our relationships have rankings or levels based on how dedicated two people are. Is it only a crush? Are you in a relationship? Best buddies? Boyfriend/girlfriend? Partners? Engaged? Married? Divorced? Each title shows the level of commitment in that relationship (or lack thereof). As a result, we consider this the third and final component of love.

A commitment is a decision made to and for one another. To decide to commit is to rule out all other possibilities except the one you've chosen. Without commitment, there is no true romantic relationship. You may be physically or emotionally together, but without commitment, it is not a spiritual connection. With a level of commitment that you feel comfortable and secure in, growth occurs and a new healthy relationship can emerge.

Commitment makes everything possible because it provides a secure environment in which everything else can thrive. We can drop our walls, stop defending our identity and limiting beliefs, and change can arise. It allows your partner to be a safe space for you—a place where you can speak, free of criticism, judgment, or threatening actions. You can mess up without them wanting to break up with you every time you are less than perfect. This gives a level of security, between the good and the bad times; a sense of certainty that you have a partner by your side who loves you, supports you, and will stay with you no matter what.

In fact, commitment is the ingredient that transforms your relationship into a partnership because it creates the assurance that you will always have each other's back. Even if you both make mistakes, bicker, or change, you're committed to each other, which means you won't give up. When two people commit to the same goal (like having a healthy relationship), everything becomes easier, and you can trust they will be there for you, as a teammate would. This is a partnership, which has a very different dynamic than a relationship.

If the desire fades and the affection is absent, what remains is commitment. It is not the foundation, but it is what will make or break a romantic relationship. It is the most difficult ingredient to achieve and the most dangerous to lose. When you break commitments to your partner, you lose trust and thus intimacy. Where there is no intimacy, there is never as much passion, because who wants to put their entire body, mind, and soul into the hands of someone they don't trust? No one!

However, it is preferable to combine commitment with another ingredient, such as affection or desire. Commitment alone is boring. Imagine any food with just salt and no other seasonings for the rest of your life? It can get pretty bland.

If this persists over time, and there is no passion or affection, then cheating or wandering can happen since humans do not live in a vacuum. If someone else comes along and supplies your partner with something you don't give them, like interest (intimacy) or desire (passion), then they might stray. As a result, it is best to show them more than just commitment. Giving them what they need along with passion and affection is how you can gain more commitment and prevent unnecessary straying.

Although we are not saying that it is ok to stray under any circumstances, it is just more likely to happen when one or both partners are not getting enough passion or affection from each other.

Whether they stray or not, with only commitment, it can feel like a lifeless relationship where two people are just withering away in monotony. They may stay together, but only out of sheer routine or comfort. Neither this nor straying are ideal situations. So, it is vital to have more than just commitment for it to feel like a healthy relationship.

Commitment can take many forms. What you're willing to offer and receive can influence your level of commitment. One couple may commit to being monogamous, but another couple may commit to being polygamous. Neither is correct or incorrect. They are both commitments, but two different types of "connecting."

Before you continue reading, there is something vital to remember. In the scuba-diving world, divers adhere to the rule of going as slow as the slowest swimmer. A similar rule applies to love. With relationships, it is the person who provides the least amount of ingredients who sets the pace. In fact, the person with the least commitment makes the final decision on what level the relationship will remain at. You can't make the other person want more commitment; therefore, you must move at the pace that makes them comfortable. For example, if you want to marry someone but they aren't ready, you won't get married because the relationship is progressing at the pace of the person with the least commitment, which is them at that point.

Commitment can take longer for one person than another to feel in their bones. To satisfy their partner or family, people commit before they are ready, which leads to resentment or bitterness from feeling coerced or manipulated. When you ask for commitment, make sure you (and they) aren't just doing it for social, moral, or religious reasons. You should be committing because it's what you want, and your soul is ready for it.

In Chapters 5, 6, and 7, we will discuss how to increase commitment, desire, and affection. Before that, in Chapter 4, we will go into further detail about the different recipes that are created depending on the "ingredients" in a relationship. Are you ready to discover which recipe represents your relationship?

Before we dive into the eight different "recipes" of love, here is an opportunity for you to show love...

∞

Your Opportunity To Help Others

Help others discover that strong, long-lasting passion and intimacy can last beyond the "honeymoon" stage of relationships.

> *"To serve one is to serve all."*
>
> - The Law of One, Carla Rueckert

You may recall from the introduction that we have a loving, committed, and passionate relationship today because we laid the groundwork for a meaningful relationship both before and after we met.

We have always sought to expand our knowledge of relationships and share the wisdom that has worked wonders in our own partnership.

Help us share this knowledge and experience with others so that they can have more of what we all truly desire—love. If you have found any value in this book so far, please share your findings with others.

Simply by telling them how this book helped you and what they can expect to find inside, you'll help them understand that love isn't just a feeling. It requires action and an unwavering desire to move forward.

By leaving a review on Amazon for this book, you'll help other couples revive their relationships and reignite the spark that drew them together in the first place. You can leave a review by using this link: https://bit.ly/Review-L2L

Thank you for helping us serve others more!

Chapter 4

Roommates, Cellmates, or Soulmates

Relationships generate a variety of flavors depending on the amount of each of the three ingredients you have, just like a cooking recipe. This chapter will help you understand where you're at so you can move closer to your desired level or "recipe" of love. You'll understand what level your relationship is at right now based on the amounts of affection, passion, and commitment you have. You'll also learn how to take it to the next step or all the way to the ultimate healthy relationship, by becoming soulmates.

Each recipe has several methods to love someone. There are many types of relationships in our lives, including strangers, acquaintances, friendships, families, and significant others. Based on the three elements, each form of relationship has a different level of love. We will explain all eight recipes in detail.

It's important to note that if you're in a specific "recipe," it doesn't mean you're locked there. You can develop certain practices to add intimacy, passion, or commitment to the relationship to advance up the ladder. It's difficult to remove an ingredient from a recipe once it's added. It's much easier to put in a bit, mix it, taste it, then decide if you want to add more. After we go over the eight recipes, you'll learn how to awaken each ingredient in your relationship, whether they have been there before or you wish to experience them for the first time together.

#1: The Cellmates = No Ingredients

Have you ever eaten food with no seasoning, spices, or sauces? It's bland! When you pass someone on the street, there is no affection, passion, or commitment, hence there is no connection, relationship, or love. It is acceptable and not unusual to share no ingredients with people we refer to as strangers or even acquaintances. However, in romantic relationships, this is not an optimal recipe.

If it's a normal recipe for strangers, why are we referencing this scenario among relationship types? What happens when two people get forced to live together because of an (unwanted) arranged marriage, a lack of resources, the need for a place to live, and so on? Consider someone in prison. Do they have a say in whom they room with? No. Since they didn't get the choice, many of them fight or stab each other because they feel forced to live with someone they don't like. As a result, when a couple lives with someone for whom they have no affection, passion, or commitment, they become what we call Cellmates. Most people wish to avoid a situation like this.

It's important to understand that being in the Cellmates situation isn't a bad thing. You don't have to feel affection, passion, or commitment toward someone all the time. If someone is Cellmates with a person they live with, it shows that they have an acquaintance or a stranger with them.

The advantage of being Cellmates is that this is the simplest recipe to transform. All you have to do is season the plain dish with some flavoring (a.k.a. ingredients), which we will discuss in later chapters. Each of the following three recipes has at least one ingredient.

#2: The Friend Zone = Affection Only

Have you ever been friend-zoned by someone you like? The Friend Zone, noted for affection but lacking passion or commitment, refers to a friendship rather than a romantic relationship. A person feels warm when they're with someone and are at ease in their company, but don't want to advance into a serious relationship with that person.

If one of the two people wants passion and commitment but the other does not, this combination is not ideal. A good example is when a teenage boy has a crush (a.k.a. desire) on one of his female friends. Yet, she does not know and doesn't feel the same way for him. He waits for the moment her boyfriend breaks her heart so he can swoop in and save her, run off into the sunset, and live happily ever after. This rarely happens, and she might perceive his advances as weird or a complete shock, resulting in a loss of friendship. If the boy has affection and passion for the girl, but she does not have affection and passion for him, the relationship remains in the Friend Zone. This can only change if she develops passion and/or commitment for him.

It's also worth noting that a relationship only progresses from Cellmates to Friend Zone when both parties develop fondness for and acceptance of each other. If they refuse to accept the other person for who they are, they will stay as Cellmates. For example, if someone says, "After getting to know her more, I realized I couldn't stand her personality," no affection or relationship can develop.

#3: The Booty Call = Passion Only

The Booty Call occurs when two people feel passion for each other but no affection or commitment. Since there is no affection, they don't go on dates, they don't hold hands, and they don't meet each other's parents. However, they sure know how to rock each other's world in bed. Even though they feel hot for each other, the relationship doesn't last long because there is no commitment.

There are many reasons one or both members of the duo bring no other ingredients. Maybe one or both is/are in another relationship (which would be cheating in this context). Or they may not feel safe enough (or trusting enough) to share a home or their deepest secrets with the other person. Also, they might not be looking for or ready for anything more than a passionate one-night stand (a.k.a. Booty Call).

There are also many cases in which one person feels only passion, but the other person feels passion yet wants affection *and* commitment. Take this example: a woman is sleeping with a married man at work. She feels passion but desires affection and/or commitment. He swears he will leave his wife but never does. He leaves after sex and does not stay to converse or cuddle with her, leaving her with the impression that something is missing. She may understand that he will never leave his wife for her. She can stay and continue as the Booty Call, or she can leave him and find someone who feels more than passion for her and is ready to offer her the other two ingredients.

Unless both parties feel the same way, we still consider it a Booty Call scenario. It is up to the person who wants "more" to stay or leave. As stated, the person who brings the least amount of ingredients to the table will set the pace of the relationship.

#4: The Roommates = Commitment Only

The partners in such a relationship with only commitment are roommates rather than lovers; they happen to share a roof and possibly a bed. They may have had passion and affection in the past, but at this point, they are simply cohabiting. They might kiss each other for a second and say hello when they pass each other in the hall. Yet, they hardly get intimate together, and no one would describe them as "hot" for each other. You wouldn't catch this couple making out in the hall or pinching each other's butt when no one is looking. Most starving couples are in this phase, and it is not the kind of story that happens in fairy tales.

Examples of people who commit to each other but lack affection or passion are a roommate with whom you are courteous but not connected to. You are present in each other's life but not close or involved with each other, apart from sharing a space. When this occurs in love relationships, we refer to them as Roommates, because the interaction is similar. They coexist because of a commitment they have made, such as marriage or agreeing to stay together "for the kids," or at least until they grow up, but there is no spice or sweetness!

This is the stage at which one, or both, people may cheat. They may be married but live as Roommates. So, when someone else shows them passion and/or affection, it can grow into an emotional and/or physical affair. They are now receiving what their partner was not providing. This is a recipe for disaster.

#5: The Friends With Benefits = Affection + Passion

The Friends With Benefits relationship has affection, hence the "friends," and passion, hence the "benefits," but the pair don't take action toward commitment. It's an enjoyable ride, but nothing more. Given that there is no commitment, the relationship can end, so there is no sense of assurance or permanence.

For example, suppose a couple named Lisa and Jack have been sleeping at each other's house for a year. One day

Lisa asks the guy if she can have a drawer to put her clothes in when she comes over. Instead of being excited, Jack looks at her and says, "Why would we do that? That can complicate things." Lisa is now aware that he may never be serious enough to commit. She realizes he is leading her astray and that they are merely Friends With Benefits. As a result, Lisa must make a choice. She has the option of staying as Friends With Benefits, crossing her fingers and hoping that something will change, or moving on. Since the relationship can only progress at the rate of the person who contributes the fewest ingredients, if they are unwilling to add more affection and/or passion, you can either wait until something changes their mind or move on completely.

However, there are situations when the relationship progresses from Friends With Benefits to something more. This happens when one or both of them realize they can't live without the other and decide to commit so the relationship can continue.

#6: The Royal Wedding = Affection + Commitment

The Royal Wedding relationship forms right from the get-go or it can develop. If it started from the beginning, it's probably because at least one party member got married for status, power, money, security, safety, or stayed for their offspring. It could also be marriages that have lasted a long time but whose passion has waned, or they got together without realizing there was no sexual chemistry. A sexless marriage (having sex fewer than 10 times per year)[36] is a real possibility for these pairs.

People in this type of relationship are pals living under the same roof; there is commitment and affection but no passion or spark. This type of relationship can become more of a business agreement than a marriage. They both may miss the spontaneity and excitement of a passion filled relationship. It is possible to bring back passion into a relationship where it has faded. However, it is much harder (and not as common) to bring passion into a relationship where it never existed.

An example of this is when a woman marries a man she sees as a reliable, secure provider. Eventually, she withholds sex and refuses to be the person she acted as before they married. She closes off and ceases to be the seductive enchantress she was. These couples have sex once in a blue moon. She might do it for the sake of routine or going through the motions, or just enough to keep the man from wandering or leaving her. She may still indulge in idle conversation and connect periodically (a.k.a. show affection), but there isn't the spark that he or she once hoped for.

Whatever the case may be, increasing polarity in the relationship is a surefire way to rekindle the flames of passion, no matter how long you've been together. Not to worry, though; we'll cover all of that in Chapter 6.

#7: The Las Vegas Marriage = Passion + Commitment

When two people have a strong desire for each other, they may get married or move in together before they have developed a deep connection. Such a scenario is fantastic for a fairy tale, but passion can eventually fade in real life. Without the right practices to keep the passion alive and the time to develop a liking for your partner, you may find yourself in the Roommate Stage. A couple "trapped" by a marriage license or a new baby may come to realize that they never really knew each other, and that their relationship was nothing more than a passionate fling.

What happens in Las Vegas stays in Las Vegas, right? With over 150 weddings happening every day, Las Vegas is called, "the Marriage Capital of the World," according to the city's official website.[37] But, without affection, partners may realize they know very little about each other. Imagine what it's like to wake up with a ring on your finger and no recollection of how it got there. This may be why Nevada has the reputation as the divorce capital of the world.[38]

You've probably read or seen at least one fairy tale in which the princess falls in love with the prince at first sight and quickly marries him. The film doesn't spend much time on what happens later, but it's obvious that their unfamiliarity with one another will produce marital difficulties.

"Booty Calls" may wake up one morning with an "I'm pregnant" text message, ushering them into the Las Vegas Marriage phase. They may find themselves parenting one child, yet they aren't even close friends and have never had a conversation about parenting. They may feel sexually attracted to one another at first, but they discover they don't have the emotional connection necessary to build a lasting relationship. The couple will have a hard time developing and maintaining a good connection if they don't share common values, rules, or goals in life. It's possible, but it will take time and conscious practice.

Some people marry because they quickly fall in love with each other. They assumed that getting to know each other and feeling deeply connected would take time. Seeing as they don't know each other, they could be "in love" with an idealized version of each other rather than their true self. As a result, they may feel trapped in a relationship with someone they don't like or trust. This can make the relationship unhealthy.

You are not required to marry within the next day, week, or year if you are in a similar situation. After all, if it's built to last, there's no need to rush. You have every right to follow the natural progression of your relationship and get to know them gradually. Every relationship is unique and you should do what feels right to you; however, it is always best to get to know someone first, or you may end up like the Las Vegas Marriage.

#8: The Soulmates = Affection + Passion + Commitment

The Soulmates have all three ingredients present in their relationship, making it the type desired by most people. This is the love most people put on their vision boards or dream about in their fantasies. There is affection, so they know, like, and trust each other. Passion comes from how strongly they want each other. And, since they commit to each other, they *want* to spend the rest of their lives together.

Soulmates don't happen out of thin air the way most people think. It takes effort, like all great things in life. Going through the motions seldom creates a passionate, intimate, committed union. It can lead to boredom and a stale Roommates recipe, where the couple is so busy with life, work, and kids that they forget to prioritize their relationship. Things dissipate, until one day it's been months or even years since they had passionate sex, or stared into each other's eyes.

Realize there is no relationship on the planet in which both parties experience full intimacy 100% of the time, feel intense passion at all times, and feel committed all day, every day. It ebbs and flows, but all the ingredients are present a majority of the time. If the passion wanes, they do things to spice it up. When affection is lacking, they do things to bring more intimacy into their union. There can be times when one may want to leave, but the couple works it out because they dedicate themselves to their relationship.

If two people consider themselves Soulmates because they have all the ingredients, but they break up constantly, this isn't the Soulmates recipe. Instead, the person who leaves wants to be Friends With Benefits and will give any reason to avoid committing. To be considered Soulmates all three ingredients must be present, including commitment for both partners; breaking up is out of the question because they have committed to each other.

Sometimes relationships start with all three ingredients, but after having children or starting a business, it diminishes. No need to panic, because the rest of this book is about how to increase passion, intimacy, and commitment to have the love we all want.

Recipe Chart

What to Do Now?

What recipe is your relationship in? Whichever it is, your relationship can always move up the levels, because we're going to show you how to add more intimacy, passion, and commitment in the next few chapters. The question is, are you willing to do the work necessary to make your dream relationship come true and become Soulmates? If you are, keep reading.

Chapter 5

How to Cultivate Intimacy

∞

Did you know married people who are also best friends enjoy twice as much life satisfaction and well-being as those who are unmarried?[39] Many couples get together based on lust, only to discover that they don't like each other outside of physical attraction. This is where developing intimacy comes in. There is no true relationship without affection or intimacy. We regard affection as the primary ingredient and starting point for a relationship, because there would be no fondness or rapport without it. There is mutual liking between the two of you when intimacy establishes a relationship. That's why this ingredient is so fundamental for a long-lasting, healthy relationship.

Affection and intimacy result from knowing, liking, and accepting someone for who they are. Accepting someone implies that you care about them regardless of their flaws. Without this fundamental starting point, how can you ever get acquainted with someone or become friends with them until you know, accept, and like them? You can't, or else you'll be Cellmates or Roommates. As a result, the rest of this chapter will concentrate on how to know, like, and accept your partner to achieve more closeness.

Certain elements are necessary for intimacy. These include trust, honesty, integrity, openness, vulnerability, sincerity, and acceptance. This chapter will talk about these components and provide some practical strategies for enhancing affection to get the sweet sauce that is the basis of the Soulmates recipe.

Trust builds intimacy. If you don't trust somebody, you won't feel vulnerable or open up to them about your feelings and opinions. When someone gives you their heart and body, they trust you won't abuse or exploit them. Trust arises when you're open, honest, and vulnerable with each other. If you're upfront and honest, regardless of how people feel or what they think of you, it's up to them to accept you (or not). Once they accept you, they know they can trust you since you were upfront and honest with them, which allows them the space to be open and honest, too.

To be trusted requires more than just honesty; it requires sincerity. Sincerity comes from being free from pretense or deceit and saying what you feel or believe. This is about authenticity—being real about who you are, which requires total vulnerability and a willingness to share. This can be difficult in a world of illusions where everyone is trying to be someone else or portraying fake perfection. If you want to win their affection, you must be honest with them and with yourself about who you are and what you stand for. Trying to be someone you're not is a sign you're losing trust and respect for yourself. As simple as it may sound, being yourself is one of the quickest methods for acquiring someone's trust and acceptance.

Take the sun as an example. Does it still shine even when people complain about how hot it is? Yes. Does it continue to shine even when the Earth blocks it with clouds? Yes, since it is always shining, no matter what. Whatever people say about it, feel toward it, or think of it, the sun will stay true to its generous, radiant nature. That is authenticity.

This is where integrity comes into play, which is about being honest and having strong moral values. It also refers to the state of being whole and undivided. If you are complete, you stick to your morals and not deviate from them by acting in ways that are not your own.

The same is true for you. Do you act differently when you see someone you admire, even if they don't hold the same values as you, or do you stick to your morals? Do you change your behavior or values depending on whom you're with? Or do you remain steadfast no matter who is present or what happens? The latter requires complete awareness, acceptance, and knowledge of who you are at your core. Many people cannot grasp that the more you can be yourself and stay true to yourself, the more people will like and admire you. However, inflating your sense of self to impress others can make most people think you lack integrity and are out of touch with yourself. How could they trust or like that?

Once these fundamentals are in place, intimacy and affection may bloom because they trust you. If the other person decides not to accept or like you, that's fine, since you already know they're not for you, and you can move on. If you are already in a relationship with someone who knows, likes, and accepts you, this is when intimacy and affection-building strategies come into play.

There are five ways to increase intimacy and affection in your relationship:

- More time together
- Shared interests
- Shared experiences
- Discovering more about one another
- Physical touch

Let's go through each of these so you can sweeten your love life.

Time Together

Time fosters affection since it grows over hours, days, weeks, and longer. It is a fundamental truth of life that people trust those with whom they have spent more time than those with whom they have spent less time. The people in your life with whom you have the strongest bonds and confide in the most are likely to be the people you have spent the most time with. This is the starting point for affection because none of the other ways for growing an intimate connection would be conceivable without time together.

Usually, the best times for couples are the times when it's just the two of them for an extended time. This should happen regardless of the demands of family, children, and other responsibilities because everyone deserves time for themselves. Couples who wish to prosper must spend time alone together. After the house, kids, jobs, and pets, many couples don't share a moment together for longer than a quick post-dinner check-in or goodnight kiss. Time alone is often a game-changer in relationships.

Plan a regular date night to spend at least a few hours alone together each week. See if you can get two days alone per month with no commitments other than spending time together. It's best to get away from home because the needs of your home or family can interfere with your time together if the kids knock or something needs to be done.

Shared Interests

How do you instill affection in two people? First, go deeper than the standard, "How are you?" "I'm OK, thanks for asking" exchanges. By sharing similar interests with your partner, you form a bond. This could be as simple as similar tastes in TV shows or music. Try to take this a step further and see if there are deep topics, hobbies, dreams, desires or fantasies you have in common.

Here is an important secret... The "*what*" is important, but knowing a person's "*why*" fosters a deeper understanding of who they are. Once you've found something you both like, delve deeper. *Why* does your partner enjoy that band or that particular food? Knowing the "*why*" allows you to go deeper, discover more similarities, and develop a new level of understanding and affection for your partner.

You may also discover that, despite your shared interests, you value these things in very different ways. Let's look at how Monica and Fabio's pancake-loving relationship increased their intimacy. Monica loves pancakes because her mother used to make them every Sunday morning when the entire family was together. Fabio enjoys pancakes because it is the only type of sweet breakfast his parents allowed him to have. Although they have different reasons for loving the same thing, they can now create more intimacy by reliving these moments together. Fabio can invite the whole family over on Sunday and make pancakes for Monica as a surprise. Monica can make Fabio pancakes for dinner to bring a laugh to the table and remind him that he can have pancakes whenever he wants now. Understanding each other's "why" can bring deeper intimacy and allow you to show more affection to one another.

Shared Experiences

Without shared experiences, there is no familiarity, companionship, or relationship, let alone a soulmate. Shared experiences are great for improving closeness and affection because when you overcome an issue together, go on trips together, or do an activity together, you form a stronger bond.

Consider the people you have the strongest ties with. Have you had more encounters with them than with others? Having more shared experiences, like cooking together, or trying something new can make you feel like you've known them for longer.

It is helpful to be inventive and do things you would not do, since it encourages you to think and act differently rather than go through the motions of your normal routine. This new experience creates new neurons in your brain, which creates new emotional ties. As discovered by researchers at MIT, the brain rewires itself through plasticity in response to changing behavioral condition s.[40]

Remember that the more emotional the encounter, the more affection there is. When we say "shared experiences," we mean ones where both people have fun, because this is a sign of a positive relationship. In her book,

Play Solution, Jeanette Lauer says, "Having fun together can help couples feel positive emotions, which can increase relationship satisfaction..."[41]

To take this a step further, having fun is vital to relationship satisfaction. In his book, *12 Hours to a Great Marriage*, Howard Markman went as far as saying, "Some studies have even found that having fun together is the most important factor... and the greatest influence on overall marital satisfaction."[42] The advice to do things that you both consider fun applies if you're married or not. Pursue a hobby together or do something you both consider risky or different, and go have fun, because your relationship depends on it!

Discover More About Your Partner

The third technique to increase intimacy is to better understand your partner. We often become accustomed to the people in our lives, taking them for granted and losing interest in them. It occurs to the best of us, no matter who we are, because of The Law of Familiarity.[43]

Instead of asking, "How are you?" or other scripted, dull questions, it's time to ask more in-depth questions that get to the heart of what makes your partner unique. We can accomplish this by asking questions on date nights or at random times during the day out of a desire to get to know your partner better.

In Chapter 2, we listed lots of questions to understand your partner's needs, values, rules, and more. Use those questions, as well as the ones below, to get to know them better. The next prompts are some conversation starters that may teach you something new about your partner and break the Law of Familiarity.

Conversation Starters

- When you were a kid, what did you dream of being or doing?
- What are your goals in life? How can I support you in meeting those goals?
- What brings a big smile to your face?
- What do you love to talk about?
- What would you like to learn more about?
- If you had extra time, what would you do with it?
- If we went on a vacation today, where would you want to go?
- What would be your ideal life in 5, 10, or even 20 years?

- What's one thing most people don't know about you?
- What is your greatest fantasy?
- What would you do with your life if money were not a concern?
- What emotions do you avoid most?
- What emotions do you want to feel most?
- What is life about for you?
- How do you know someone loves you?
- What must a person never do in a relationship?
- What do you desire most?
- What's abundant in your life?
- Who are you at your core?
- What do you fear most?
- What has to happen for you to feel loved?
- Fill in the blank: Life is ___.

Another great way to learn more about your partner is through personality tests. They offer one of the greatest ways to learn about yourself and your partner, because why not find out what you can do to maximize your personality and potential? There are likely aspects of your partner that you'd like to know on a deeper level. This is your chance to discover their strengths and their sticking points.

Also, keep in mind that if a personality test brings up elements that don't match what your partner is like, just ignore those. No personality test can account for all the complexities of a human being. So, use this method as a way of understanding them better, not as a strict set of traits you expect them to abide by at all times.

Here are a few tests we've used over the years to get to know each other better, and help us as individuals in our personal evolution.

- Myers Briggs 16 Personality Tests: www.16personalities.com/free-personality-test[6]
- Clifton's StrengthsFinder 2.0:www.gallup.com/cliftonstrengths/en/254033/strengthsfinder.aspx[7]
- Authentic Happiness Index by the University of Pennsylvaniawww.authentichappiness.sas.upenn.edu/testcenter[8]
- Life Path Number by Dan Millman:www.peacef

ulwarrior.com/life-purpose-calculator/[9]

- Enneagram by George Gurdijieff:www.truity.com/test/enneagram-personality-test[10]

Physical Touch

Since we only touch and allow contact from folks we know, like, and trust, physical touch is a sign of increased affection. It fosters bonding between couples thanks to the oxytocin surges that arise from it. It also lowers cortisol (stress hormone), and all you need is the power of a hug to get the benefits.[49] Sometimes a hug isn't necessary; a simple touch of the small of their back, arm around the shoulder, or simply holding hands can increase the closeness of your union.

However, it is important to be cautious. A person's responsiveness to touch changes depending on how they feel and their level of comfort with you. There are two key elements to consider regarding touch: time and sensory acuity.

According to an NLP World article, sensory acuity is the ability to be acutely aware of detail in front of you.[50] Use this to read people's body language and determine whether they are ready and willing to be touched at each moment. If you touch someone more than they feel comfortable with, or when they do not want to be touched, it could backfire. If you approach them, do they move closer to you, or do they back away? Do they extend their hand for a handshake when you reach for a hug? This reflects their level of comfort and trust in you at that moment.

Timing is also important when deciding whether to touch someone. If you or your partner is sweaty and dirty, consider whether they want to be hugged in the same way as when you are both clean. They may also be unwilling to be touched for a variety of personal reasons. If they are angry, consider what touching them might do to their anger (it could make it worse). So, use timing to determine whether they are ready or willing to be touched.

If they want to be touched, touch them on the hand, shoulder, and other non-sexual areas. Allow them to ease you into more and more intimate areas. The closer you get to their belly, hips, and chest, the more sexual it becomes, so consider whether they are ready and willing for that kind of contact.

Give Them Affection the Way They Need It

Did you know that we all receive and offer love in different ways? Affection can appear as more than just "displays of affection." For example, giving them things, doing things for them, or spending time with them are other ways of showing affection.

Not everyone shows and receives affection in the same way. The way you express love to your partner may not be the way they prefer because they do not "speak" that language. For instance, you might give your partner affection through touch, but they feel more affection when you tell them with words. It's helpful to understand what they need to feel affection from you; otherwise, resentment can develop from feeling unwanted.

Dr. Gary Chapman refers to the many ways of expressing love as *The Five Love Languages*.[51] These are words of affirmation, acts of service, gifts, quality time, and physical touch. Couples often battle for years feeling unloved because neither partner understands how to express their love to the other in a "language" they can connect with.

One way you can give your partner affection in their favorite way is by figuring out which language they "speak" best using *The Love Language Quiz*. Giving your partner love in the way they best receive it will make a world of difference, be that words, gifts, acts, touch, or time.

Use *The Love Language Quiz* to find out their love language (and yours), so that you can shower them with the type of love they receive best.[52]

Journal Prompts

- What are your top two Love Languages?
- How can your partner meet your top two Love Languages daily, weekly, and monthly?
- What are your partner's top two Love Languages?
- How can you meet your partner's top two Love Languages daily, weekly, and monthly? (Feel free to ask them to get more accurate results and write down the answers)

Using the various methods discussed in this chapter, you can cultivate more intimacy and affection, which can increase closeness and a sense of trust and acceptance of one another. However, this is not enough to make your relationship whole because relying on just intimacy and affection can lead to a lackluster relationship. As a result, in the following chapter, we will discuss how to increase passion for a desire-filled relationship.

Chapter 6

How to Enhance Passion

∞

Passion is the element that spices up a relationship, since it adds life and flavor. There are various definitions of passion, but we'll use The Britannica Dictionary's definition: "a strong sexual or romantic feeling for someone."[53] Passion is one of the hardest ingredients of love to keep consistent. This is why we recommend certain practices to keep desire flowing, to raise attraction, and to add zest to your relationship.

Some ways to raise desire and passion are:

1. Increase Polarity
2. Space and Time Apart (don't worry, we're not talking about breaking up)
3. The Importance of Variety (change in environ-

ment, behavior, or attire)

4. Self-Improvement

Let's look at each of these.

Increase Polarity

Chemistry between couples causes polarity, which is required before desire awakens. According to the Law of Polarity, everything has its opposite.[54] When the light goes out, you know it's dark. If there is an up, there must also be a down. For there to be one thing, there must be another. Since opposites attract, a magnet attracts its energetic opposite.

When we say "opposites attract," we don't just mean men and women. We're also mentioning feminine and masculine energy. In terms of traits and behaviors, masculine energy is the polar opposite of feminine energy. It differs from the assigned male or female sex definition in that both females and males have masculine and feminine energy. Men can have feminine characteristics, and women can have masculine characteristics.[55] We all have a different percentage of each energy center that can change over time.

The masculine and feminine polarities are dance partners who cannot exist apart. They are opposite in every way. The masculine is linear and structured, whereas the feminine is fluid and cyclical; the masculine is active and expansive, whereas the feminine is passive and yielding. They are opposites, which is a good thing because it ignites the fire that sparks desire, attraction, and passion in the relationship.

No one is only feminine or only masculine; everyone has qualities of both and is a mix of the two. However, most people lean toward one polarity more than the other, so one is more dominant than the other. Often, but not always, it is the essence you were born with. If you were born more determined and active, you are most likely more masculine at heart. If you were born more free-spirited, talkative, and expressive, you might be more feminine at heart.

If you are predominantly masculine, you will attract a more feminine partner. If you are predominantly feminine, you will attract a more masculine partner. The less masculine you are, the less feminine your partner will be, and vice versa. Like batteries, it must balance both poles to generate "electricity." Just like a battery has a negative and positive side, our relationships have opposites as well. This generates equilibrium, which is both necessary and inherent in all of creation.

The more each polarity embraces its essence, the stronger the attraction. The more balanced each polarity becomes, the less attraction there is because the strength of the opposing poles is low. Just like a magnet that is 50% positive and 50% negative, it does not create a powerful pull from another magnet. Consider a Roommates relationship—the couple has spent so much time together that they balance each other out. Do you see these couples jumping each other's bones? Most likely not. Polarizing further into your natural essence is beneficial because it will increase your desire for each other.

Gender has nothing to do with masculine or feminine polarities. It's not about the sexual organs or hormones either, but about the energy the person produces. Most men are higher in masculine energy while most women are higher in feminine energy, but that doesn't mean the contrary doesn't exist. You can be a mostly masculine person if you are a woman, or a more feminine person if you are a man. If they feel good in that role, is there anything wrong with it? Of course not, because it's only an issue if it doesn't feel natural or good to them.

For the sake of ease, while speaking about masculine and feminine energy, we will use the pronouns "they/them/theirs" as well as Alison Armstrong's references of "hunters" as masculine energy and "gatherers" as feminine energy to honor the fact that masculine and feminine energy is gender-neutral and can be found in every person.[56] We may give examples of women and men that show qualities of feminine and masculine energy for the sake of better understanding how gatherers and hunters are in real life, but please be aware that these are just examples and do not mean that the energies cannot be found in other genders. We are giving examples for the purposes of understanding and learning in ways we believe may be supportive.

If you wish to boost desire in your partner, the first step is to become more polarized toward your natural essence, whether masculine or feminine. There are different things you can do to make your relationship more polarized and, as a result, increase your desire and passion for each other. We will work with each essence on how to polarize further and recommend that you read both sections, regardless of your innate nature.

Tips to Polarize the Masculine

Think of masculine energy as the hunter. As a result, when the masculine partner does activities that are more hunter-like, they will further polarize. Nowadays, these daily activities will differ from the traditional "hunting" activities performed by our ancestors. Modern equivalents of hunter behavior could include:

- Being with other masculine individuals

- Seeking a mission, purpose, or outcome
- Making decisions
- Overcoming problems (a.k.a. conquering)
- Providing, protecting, and building
- Pursuing freedom in some form

These are some ways the masculine could further polarize into more masculine energy.

Time With Other Hunters

When hunters interact with other hunters, they all get more polarized because they are all firing each other up just by being around each other. We become like others around us because of energy.

So, when they come together, what do they do? They will often be active, such as playing sports or achieving outcomes together. When they communicate, it's often about a handful of things: this includes solutions to overcome obstacles, a mission, things they have defeated (such as an addiction), sports (a.k.a. freedom), or their partners (a.k.a. providing and protecting). This nourishes the masculine essence and further polarizes them. Spending time with other masculine people will allow a hunter to return home ready to ravish the gatherer with passion.

Having Purpose and Making Decisions

Having a goal, mission, or something that gives you purpose in life is one of the most important things you can do to become more masculine. A purpose requires focus and organization because it has a goal and a deadline. Focus and structure are masculine characteristics because they are linear, as is the masculine. Scheduling and arranging your desk, space, or day are all activities that can help you maintain organization in your life and hence be more masculine.

If you want to reach a certain goal, you have to make decisions and act quickly. This requires saying no to one thing in order to get another. When you focus on just one thing, you are strengthening your masculine qualities.

The problem with many hunters today is that they work in jobs they hate. It's more of a chore than a mission, so even if they "work" 40 hours a week, their relationships are bland because they are not seeking their life's purpose. As a result, their gatherer senses their lack of commitment to a larger cause. The gatherer will then have to assume the masculine role and develop their own sense of purpose or drive. If one individual does not assert masculinity, the other finds it difficult to feel their femininity.

You've perhaps seen similar scenarios in your life, where a couple lacks passion and sexual chemistry because of this dynamic. This can lead to boredom, complacency, or resentment. If enough time passes, they may end up as Roommates or even Cellmates, which is far from ideal for a passionate love life.

Overcome Challenges

When hunters overcome obstacles, it develops their willpower and determination, both of which are masculine characteristics. How do hunters commonly reply when faced with a challenge, such as someone telling them they can't do something? "You just watch, and I'll show you I can." If you're a hunter, set goals for yourself and achieve them. It doesn't matter if the challenge is a job deadline or climbing a treacherous mountain; the only thing that matters is that you are attempting to overcome it.

Providing, Protecting, and Building

The masculine gains strength by providing, protecting, and building. The masculine is on the hunt, looking for their next meal so they can feed themselves and their family; there is a desire to give and provide for the feminine, who is gathering and receiving. Hunters must feed their families and provide for them, but to trap a hog or catch a fish, they must make tools.

They also want to ensure they keep their families safe from predators while they are out hunting by creating a home that will shelter and protect their partner and children. Any kind of building, especially if it will provide for and protect others, will polarize them; this includes building, working, or even taking up a hobby like construction, which will contribute to the masculine polarization. If the object you're making will provide for and protect others, it will make you feel even more polarized as a hunter.

Freedom-Focused

Since the masculine is the one who seeks the feminine, and freedom is inherent in the feminine, the masculine is always seeking both the feminine and freedom. Most "freedom fighters" are more masculine. They have a more active, assertive personality, which are hunter attributes that develop when someone fights for what they most desire. So, engaging in activities that make the hunter feel freer (which is subjective and depends on the individual) will further polarize them into the masculine. Many hunters love adventure and thrill-seeking activities because this gives them a sense of freedom that they can't get in a cubicle or office.

All these methods can polarize the hunter into a more masculine person. However, for this to work and for mutual desire to exist, the gatherer must likewise polarize into their feminine, so here are tips on how to do that after the following journal prompts.

Journal Prompts

- For the masculine: What day each week will you make time to be with other hunters?
- For the masculine: What are ways you can bring more challenges into your life?
- For the masculine: What is your purpose in life?
- For the masculine: What goals do you have for your life?
- For the masculine: What are ways you can start being more decisive?
- For the masculine: What are ways you can seek more freedom in your life?
- For the masculine: What are ways you can provide, protect, and build for others?
- For the feminine: How can you support the hunter in your life to live in a way that makes them more masculine?
- For the feminine: How can you support the

hunter to have more time with other hunters?

Tips to Polarize the Feminine

To polarize more as a gatherer requires relaxing into the feminine. It is not possible to work one's way into the feminine because it would be counterproductive. Doing is masculine, and femininity is about being. When a gatherer can't accept their feminine energy, their femininity, sexual drive, and overall happiness all suffer. Fortunately, there are some techniques that can help anyone become more feminine.

Every one of us carries feminine energy within ourselves, also known as "yin" energy. This energy moves in cycles, is flexible, empathic, vulnerable, intuitive, open, creative, compassionate, caring, and works well with others. Did you know that the more you embody your femininity, the more ease, radiance, and joy you will have? Here are some tips to help you feel more at ease and radiant.

Relaxing and De-stressing

In Chinese culture, the yin part of the yin-yang symbol is the feminine part that pulls us inward. The yang part of the yin-yang symbol is the masculine energy, which is dynamic and charging, whereas the feminine energy is passive and recharging.[57] Entering our own feminine energy is a way to refresh and rebuild. The only way to recharge is to relax and rest.

But how can you unwind? Try doing some self-love rituals after work to shift from a masculine focus of getting things done to a more feminine focus on being and feeling. You could run a hot bath, grab a book and a cup of tea, or light a candle and listen to relaxing music while doing some yoga, stretching, or self-massage. Anything that helps you transition and get into a more relaxed and feeling state will help you polarize into a more feminine essence.

It is OK to give yourself the time to relax, especially after being in hunting mode all day, even if other obligations need your attention. If they realize it, the hunter in your life will appreciate how radiant you are after taking the time to relax and take care of yourself. You will have more energy to care for others when you take the time to recoup and rest your body and mind.

Slowing down is another excellent method to unwind. If your mind races, meditate or sing a favorite song to calm down. Take deep breaths and center yourself back into your body if you feel your overstimulated nervous system building up. If you're going through a stressful time, put on fuzzy socks and snuggle into a soft warm blanket. There are countless ways to de-stress. What's important is finding your favorite method and using it when you want to relax into the feminine.

Give Yourself More Time and Drop the To-Do List

Masculine energy powers most of our modern-day society. Things like to-do lists, deadlines, and outcomes. If you want to polarize into your feminine as a gatherer, you must get rid of the masculine demands when you return home following a long day. You can try to relax, as we suggested earlier, but if there is a timer, deadline, or list of results you need to accomplish, relaxation isn't likely. To relax, there must be no time constraints or schedules.

When you go home from a day of doing and hunting, make time to just be and realize that we are human beings, not human doings. Put your to-do list aside, switch off the timer, and experience your five senses: taste, touch, smell, sight, and sound. We refer to this as "going with the flow," a feminine concept that means to allow whatever comes and goes without securing a certain outcome or meeting a deadline. Alison Armstrong refers to this as "puttering."[58] Try it today. Turn off the timer, give yourself extra time, put your list aside, and do anything you feel like, even if it takes longer and is in no particular order.

The word feeling is feminine because the masculine is the one who thinks and rationalizes, whereas the feminine is the one who is feeling and being. Before you plan everything for when you get home, just go with whatever seems right at the moment. This will help you relax into your feminine. If you planned to do yoga, but when you get home you feel like opening a bottle of wine and sitting in a bath, do it and forget about your previous plans or lists.

Creative Energy

Creative energy is feminine energy. In a spiritual sense, our creative and sexual energy comes from within the sacral chakra, womb space, or energy center. Feeling creative or sexual "opens" us up (not just our legs but our hearts, too) while supporting our mental health. Studies by Tamara A. Shella of the Cleveland Clinic Art Therapy Department reveals that art therapy improves mood and reduces pain and anxiety.[59] Throughout history, gatherers have found rhythmic hand gestures to be relaxing and creative. They have gathered and created in various ways, including weaving, crocheting, stitching, and embroidery. You can include these in your day-to-day activities, as well as dancing, sketching, writing, DIY projects, and cooking, to channel your creative energy.

Your choice of artistic expression will not polarize you towards the feminine unless you have no expectations about how it will turn out. Needing a result is a masculine quality. The idea is to avoid having any expectations by remaining relaxed and flowing. You may, instead, teach your brain to seek the beauty in your creations and in life, no matter how they turn out. Finding beauty in everything, including your own creations and bodies, can help gatherers polarize even more.

Receiving

Feminine energy is all about receiving. If someone offers you a cup of tea, practice accepting it and telling them you received it with affection. This might be as simple as looking them in the eyes with a smile and saying "thank you," or as grand as a hug. The key is to receive without feeling obligated to always give back.

When trying to polarize more toward the feminine, it's important to acknowledge the masculine force and let it give. Masculine energy provides and protects. Receiving from others, especially hunters, enables them to feel appreciated and loved. It can make them want to give you more to earn your praise. We're not just talking about receiving gifts. Acknowledging someone for opening a door for you, sharing something with you, listening to you, or thinking about you is an example of this concept. Opening a pickle jar or asking someone to help bring the grocery bags into the house allows them to give, which puts you in the position to receive. Receiving is an act that can help you feel feminine, as is bonding with others.

Bonding

Once upon a time, gatherers would wander the forests looking for fruit. When they returned, they had to tell their tribe members where to find those same berries, when they were in season, which ones to avoid, and so on. Alison Armstrong calls these "meadow reports."[60] For this reason, the feminine desires to connect and bond with others.

The feminine connects by bonding, empathizing, receiving, and accepting. Bonding with someone is easier when you accept and receive them as they are. Listening, holding space, and allowing them to share in a safe container—your safe container—allows them to process their emotions. Take the time to connect and be with others, because this will fulfill the need for bonding that is so innate for the feminine.

Nurture

Feminine energy looks for ways to connect with, include, care for, and nurture things. Gatherers would stay at home with their children while the hunters went in quest of food. As they cared for their family, they had to attend to their own needs to avoid becoming ill or dying, which could cease their lineage. Nurturing yourself, your family, and your partner are all important for increasing feminine energy.

Finding something or someone to nurture and care for can polarize the feminine, especially if that something or someone is your relationship. Care for your partner when they are tired. Feminine energy refuels and strengthens masculine energy. When you care for them, you help them create energy for the next hunt (or day's labor).

What is more nurturing than "Mother Earth" herself?

Nature

Have you ever observed that we refer to this planet as "Mother Earth" in various cultures? When we refer to the earth, we say "she" has a feminine essence. With this in mind, have you ever gone into nature and felt healed? In Japan, there is something known as "forest bathing" (visiting a forest and breathing its air), which they call Shinrin-yoku. Researchers have found that shinrin-yoku has a positive impact on immune function, cardiovascular and metabolic parameters,[61] physical and psychological health,[62] and stress.[63] The microbes in the soil from forest floors contribute to the feelings of relaxation and rejuvenation from nature. A systematic review found that forest bathing "significantly enhances people's emotional state, attitude, and feelings towards things... and obvious alleviation of anxiety and depression."[64]

Not only can forests provide healing, but negative ions from waterfalls and sea beds offer healing from Mother Nature that can help the feminine recharge. Dr. Philipp Eduard Anton von Lenard, a Nobel Prize winner, confirmed that negative ions (i.e., anions) are in high concentrations at sea sides and in the basins of waterfalls.[65] Why are negative ions important? They are the reason nature often puts us in a better mood. A literature review and meta-analysis on the effects of air ions on mood concluded negative ions can improve mood by lowering depression.[66]

If you want to integrate your feminine energy, spend more time in nature and find methods to incorporate natural features into your own life. Visit forests and engage in forest bathing, or spend time near waterfalls or the ocean to inhale the negative ions. This can heal and refresh your soul and rejuvenate your feminine essence. Another natural way to connect to your feminine energy is through cyclical living.

Cyclical Living

Cyclical living is a way of life that connects to the rhythms surrounding us that last over 28 days, such as seasons, moon cycles, and menstrual cycles. Tracking their periods, a.k.a. menstrual cycles, allows females to get in touch with their bodies. Females have a natural infradian menstrual cycle[67] that comprises the following stages:

- Follicular
- Ovulation
- Luteal
- Menstruation

They can follow this by tracking the cycles of the earth and the moon. The earth goes through four seasons: spring, summer, fall, and winter. The moon also has four major phases: waxing, full, waning, and new. Women's menstrual cycles followed the moon's cycles for millennia, especially before birth control.

See the pattern here? All three types of feminine energy (menstrual, earth, and moon) follow a natural cycle of increase and decrease. Functional nutritionist and women's hormone expert Alisa Vitti says the menstrual cycle lasts about 28 days for women assigned female at birth and affects six body systems, including the brain, immune system, and reproductive system.[68]

Biologically, men have a cycle, too. It's a 24-hour cycle known as the circadian rhythm, which aligns with the sun. The feminine flows differently than the masculine and follows a different cyclical beat. For example, women with female biochemistry have a 25% alteration in their brains over the course of a month. Their metabolism fluctuates based on the time of the month, how they eat, and how they exercise during each week (or reproductive phase).[69]

The lunar cycle doesn't just affect women; it appears to have an impact on specific incidents all over the world. For example, hospital admissions, traffic accidents, crimes, and even suicides increase during certain parts of the lunar phase. Research by the Department of Experimental Therapy in Poland shows that hospital staff and police officers know that during the full moon, levels of abuse and crime surge.[70] Wouldn't this imply that we're all affected by the cycles around us? When gatherers accept the flow rather than fight it, they may connect more deeply with their feminine energy and embrace how specific cycles might affect them in their everyday lives.

Time With Other Gatherers

Your inner feminine energy expands when you spend time with others in their feminine state. Throughout history, women have gathered in red tents or moon lodges during the new and full moons. In these sisterhood circles, women would connect, bleed, weave, give birth, bond, and share in a relaxed state.[71]

You can polarize toward the feminine by spending time with those who are working on bringing out their own feminine energy. Get friends to gather with, exchange tales with, or weave with. This doesn't have to be in person, you can join an online or in-person Red Tent sisterhood. A great example is *Red Tent Goddess*, which is reintroducing women's circles to the online and offline worlds with a modern-day twist.[72]

Journal Prompts

- For the feminine: How will you relax and de-stress when you get home today?
- For the feminine: How can you give yourself more time to just be?
- For the feminine: In what ways or activities can you use your creative energy?
- For the feminine: How can you practice receiving more?
- For the feminine: What other gatherers can you make time to bond with this week?
- For the feminine: How can you nurture yourself,

your partner, and others?

- For the feminine: When will you spend time in nature each day or week?
- For the feminine: How can you incorporate cyclical living into your life to get closer to your body, your cycles, and the moon?
- For the feminine: When will you spend time with other gatherers each week?
- For the masculine: How can you support your gatherer in relaxing and de-stressing when they get home?
- For the masculine: How can you take things off their plate so they can get rid of the to-do list and deadlines?
- For the masculine: How can you support your gatherer in spending more time with other gatherers?

Space and Time Apart

Space and time are two more requirements for passion to grow. If two people love each other, they must allow each other room for the desire to blossom between them.

Consider cake. If you ate cake every day, would it be as delicious as if you had it only on your birthday? No! People have a strong preference for foods that they don't often have. Hunger fuels the desire. So, allow each other some distance. When you are apart (and the duration varies depending on the relationship), the passion grows stronger than before.

Have you ever tried fasting? Do you remember how nice your first meal tasted after 48–72 hours of no food? Heck, even 12 hours of fasting makes vegetables seem sweet. In a similar way, spending time apart can benefit you both. Take your time experimenting with how long you and your partner must be apart for passion to reignite. It could be a few hours or a few days. Whatever time you have, know that it's acceptable to be away! Take advantage of your alone time and enjoy the things you love. Even if you separate for a few hours, you can keep the passion alive and prevent it from fading.

Giving each other space also allows you to work on yourself and become independent. Your partner chose you because they liked who you were before they met you. When embarking on a relationship, many people stop working on their interests and passions and start focusing on each other. That's lovely, but only for a short time. Of course, you want the honeymoon stage to last as long as possible, but to keep that passion alive, you must keep *yourself* alive. This means going about your life without your partner from time to time; by giving yourself space to do what you love, it makes you your own unique human being (instead of a copy of your partner).

The Importance of Variety

Adding variety to your life is another approach to boosting desire and passion. Anything that breaks someone's pattern introduces an element of the unexpected. Surprises of any size, big or small, ordinarily work. These don't have to be elaborate affairs; they can be as simple as a note or as grand as a vacation for just the two of you. Begin with baby steps and work your way up.

Breaking your typical routine and taking a second to hug your partner while they are doing the dishes or setting up the rooms with candles are some examples of how you can sprinkle variety along your day with little extra time or effort. If you leave the house with a quick kiss and an "I love you" before heading out the door, try saying something different next time. For example, you can say, "I know I haven't mentioned this in a while, but I hope you realize I feel so lucky to have you," then kiss your lover.

It doesn't even have to be something you say or an element of your routine; it could be where you go, for example, visiting a different restaurant for lunch. Knowing the menu and the personnel like the back of your hand lacks originality or a challenge. This can become boring after a while, much like eating the same meal every day. So, try going somewhere that involves taking a different route, learning a new menu, using different lingo, seeing unfamiliar faces, and being in a unique environment. Your conversation will not be the same because there is too much change around you to have the same exchange of words as usual.

Romance fiction authors must keep readers guessing. Skilled writers avoid cliches like flowers, dinner dates, and the boombox scene where the man professes his love while she looks out the window. Readers have grown tired of these. Instead, authors must create unique date ideas. How do you make dates or moments unique in a book and in real life? Easy. Here are a few suggestions:

- Make it personable.
    - What is it that your lover loves to do? If they love to read, take them to a bookstore and let them pick out a book. If they love art, take them to an art museum or gallery.
- Make it specific.
    - Instead of buying them the generic flowers

    or chocolate, get them something specific to them such as their favorite pastry or snack.

- Go off script.
    - Catch them by surprise by doing something completely off script. Something like calling out of work and taking them on a day trip to somewhere they wouldn't expect on a weekday such as a theme park, national park, or outing of some kind that is not what they planned.
- Add an inside joke.
    - Maybe your first date had an inside joke that brings up old memories in it so you take them somewhere that reminds them of that joke. This brings you back to old times which cements your love for each other, and also adds humor.

Self-Improvement

Improving yourself in any way can increase your partner's desire. When you work to improve your appearance, personality, social skills, character, beingness, and so on, it shows that you are maturing and desire more for your life and yourself. "Why can't they just love me the way

I am?" you may wonder. The way we present ourselves, behave, or interact does not define who we are at our core. They fell in love with you at your core, not just your looks and the things you did.

People consistently fall in love with each other while working on themselves and doing things they enjoy or that make them unique. Things like reading, learning, trying new things, and grooming themselves in attractive ways. But what happens when most people get into relationships? They come to a halt, and they stop caring about those good habits because of children, work, school, chores, or other responsibilities. Slowly, the things that made them who they are fade away, and they either become a carbon copy of their partners or stop being who they were before the relationship. Your partner fell in love with that energetic being who was moving forward with their life, caring about their goals, and wanting more for themselves and others. When this stops, it sure can affect the passion in the relationship.

The simple fact is that if we do not grow, we will die because all living things require growth. Don't you want to give your partner your all? Do you not want to be the best acting, looking, and feeling person you can be for them because you love them? Haven't you wanted to see your partner at their best most of the time, and for them to see you at your best most of the time?

What happens if either of you stops trying or caring about yourself? Maybe you've been in this situation or seen others like it. They wake up and wear pajamas all day (even to dinner). You might see them stop shaving and become unkempt. You notice they stop working out and are at a higher weight. Perhaps they smoke or drink all day, and they don't brush their teeth or shower for more than a day. Do you want to jump their bones if any of this becomes a habit? It's neither polarizing nor energizing to witness. This is a sign that they have given up on themselves and on life.

We can get so used to being, acting, and looking a certain way that we forget to check in with ourselves. We can develop habits of eating, dressing, and thinking that do not help us look, feel, or relate to others at our best. To increase passion, begin new rituals that bring out the best in you and discontinue old ones that do not.

There are many ways to improve yourself. Things like watching a communication video or reading a new book on how to have a better relationship (like this one) can help you improve. Other ways, like starting a new workout routine or diet, or trying a new hairstyle or clothing style, can all make your lover see you differently. Didn't you look at your loved one more when they dressed up or got a haircut? What about when they learned something and felt enthusiastic about it? Didn't it make you more attracted to them because they were happier and more alive while learning about it?

This brings us to the main point of self-improvement: it is for ourselves. Losing weight or quitting smoking can boost our confidence or sense of accomplishment because we are showing hard work, discipline, and perseverance. We radiate and smile more when we feel confident, making us more appealing to those who see us. Sure, new clothes can make you more appealing to your partner, but who is the one who feels good? You're the one. That is why it is "self" improvement.

How do we determine what needs to be improved? This may be the most troublesome part because it requires vulnerability and a willingness to hear about what we need to improve. We can find out what we can work on by asking those closest to us. Perhaps your partner has been waiting for you to quit smoking or improve your manners for years. Perhaps they worry about your health and how frequently you eat fried foods. You won't know unless you ask them. It may hurt at first, but try not to be offended and instead see it as an opportunity to be better for yourself and them.

We like to ask each other, "If you were designing your dream relationship, what would I (and we) do more of and less of?" You can take what they say and do something about it, or you can ignore it; it's your life and your choice. Those closest to us may know us better than we know ourselves because they see us from the outside, whereas we can get lost in the day-to-day needs of life.

Now you know how to add intimacy and passion, you have the recipe for a close, fun, and desire-filled relationship. However, if you don't add in the final-ingredient, this closeness and desire won't last as long as you wish. If your wish is to have it all, in Chapter 7 we show you how to strengthen commitment to make your love life something your grandkids will hear about.

Journal Prompts

- How can you add variety to your relationship today?
- What will you do differently today?
- What will you do today to improve yourself?
- What day this week will you spend apart to do what you love to do?

Chapter 7

How to Strengthen Commitment

What comes to mind when you hear the word "commitment" in a relationship? The word "commitment" doesn't always seem appealing in today's day and age of endless distractions, stimuli, and change, does it? However, a relationship would not survive the first date without it. Commitment allows your relationship to progress from the first meeting to a long-term partnership. It creates unity and allows you to see each other as a team. This is the opposite of being against each other or using each other as someone to talk to or have sex with. It may not bring the hot and sensual moments of passion or the laughter and joy of affection, but it creates the partnership that permits all the other ingredients to last a lifetime.

The first step to strengthening commitment is to ask yourself what kind of commitment you want. What is the highest level of commitment that you wish to experience? Think short and long term. Are you willing to commit to a long-lasting relationship? Marriage? A promise? Civil partnership?

If you are the type of person who wants to get married, the signed legal contract that gives you the title of "husband" or "wife" might do something for you. For us, it strengthened our partnership. After being together for four years, we realized that marriage brought a whole new level of commitment, dedication, and safety that we had never felt before. Don't get us wrong—our first year of marriage was hard because we both had different ideas about what marriage meant and what it meant to be lifelong partners.

You might not be the type to get married, or you might not be ready for it yet. We know that not everyone sees marriage as the ultimate sign of commitment in their relationship. The most important thing is that your partner has the same commitment goals as you. Not because they want to please you, but because they want the same things as you. For a relationship to have a lot of commitment, we've found that the two people need to talk about their short and long-term goals. It also helps to have a conversation about the relationship's ultimate vision.

Your commitment will skyrocket if you can commit to the same things!

For now, let's focus on your current level of commitment and where you want to go (or are prepared to go). Then we'll talk about how to give your partner more of what they need so that commitment becomes inevitable.

The Levels of Commitment

The level of commitment determines the nature of your relationship. Being a couple involves more devotion than dating. Being engaged involves more commitment than a dating status entails. Recognize your current level of commitment and the level you want to reach. Have you both been honest about where you are in your relationship? If not, this is the first step before you decide to progress.

For example, ask your partner if you are a couple or just dating. If you are still just dating, ask if you are exclusive. This may seem like a scary thing to do, but it can tell you a lot about whether to move forward with them or not. If you discover they are not exclusive to you, it's up to you to decide whether you want to continue the way it is or ask for exclusivity. It is up to you to stay or go if they say no to your request. If you notice you have plenty of intimacy and/or passion but no commitment, then determine whether you want to commit in your existing relationship. No matter what the current circumstances or level are, it's important to know what the dynamic is so you're both on the same page from here on out.

Once you understand where you are now, you can decide where you want to go in the short and long term. If you are dating but want to become a couple, tell them and let them know if you want to get more serious in the future. It is important that they understand your ultimate goals because whether they want the same things will determine if it happens.

Commitment requires communication. After you've decided what level you want to reach, make sure your partner is aware of your intentions. Inform them if you plan to move in together or marry after a certain timeframe. If you don't want to commit right now, talk to them. Tell them what level of commitment you want and at what point you want it. Let them know if you want to become a more serious couple, move in together at some point, become engaged, have kids, etc. If they don't know what level of commitment you want, how can they provide that for you?

To be clear, when we say talk to them about it, we mean talk to them about it now, not nine months from now. Many relationships fail because "nothing happened" quickly enough; one partner did not mention moving in, getting engaged, or having children was part of the plan. Tell your partner what you want so they don't have to guess—they aren't mind readers.

Once you figure out the amount of commitment you want and share that with your partner, here's how to gain more commitment from them: give your partner what they need. As a result, their devotion to you will grow. When we say give them what they need, we mean their six human needs, their values, and more, which we will cover in this chapter. Thankfully, you already know what their needs and values are based on the second chapter of this book.

Before we go into how to strengthen your partnership's level of commitment, we need to understand how it manifests differently in our lives depending on our gender or sexual essence. Each gender has different needs. We are all equal, but men and women are not the same, and they should not treat each other the same. We should celebrate our differences with each other. Most women are smaller in stature, have more estrogen, have periods every month, and can bear children. This differs from most men, who are stronger, have more testosterone, and can't have children without surgery. These differences created different needs to help each procreate and survive.

Couples frequently disagree on matters that aren't about their specific differences but about the differences between their masculine and feminine polarities. Each polarity has its own set of needs and desires, and if we aren't aware of them, we may believe that it is only our partner who is the "problem." In reality, people have the same global needs, regardless of polarity. Aside from the six human needs (since we already covered those earlier), we will discuss what the hunter and gatherer within us needs to commit and how to provide it for them so that commitment is inevitable.

What the Masculine (a.k.a. Hunter) Needs to Commit

Hunters require three things because of the function they have played for thousands of years. These three factors boost their masculinity and bring out the best in them. Those three things are:

- Appreciation
- Freedom
- Openness

If they don't get these things, after a while, they might seek other ways to get them or become resentful. If you are meeting their needs, they will want more of you for longer periods of time.

Appreciation

More appreciation can do wonders for couples. This could be all that is required to alter your relationship. What comes to mind when you think of a hunter? Someone who is on the hunt, seeking tools, food, water, and fire. Their urge to find food and build a fire makes them more focused and goal-oriented. They are the providers who enjoy giving and providing for their families and communities. While out hunting, they want to ensure that their family and tribe don't get eaten by a bear or soaked by the rain. So, they build to protect their family and offer shelter.

This requires work. Show appreciation for all the work they do. Show them appreciation for the things your hunter does for you and/or your family, such as providing shelter and food. Appreciate what they contribute, and they will do more. Being rewarded right away for what they do, no matter how small or large, can reap more of that thing. Appreciate activities you want them to keep doing by showing them love in their preferred "love language." A pat on the back, making them food, giving them a gift, spending time with them, or just saying "thank you" could all be examples of showing them love.

The timing of the appreciation is more important than the type of love given. Recognize hunters for doing what hunters do, which is to provide and protect, regardless of how subtle or noble the activity.

Avoid criticism at all costs, because it is the opposite of appreciation. The masculine will fold and fall in the face of stinging criticism, even if it comes as coaching or help. We're sure you've seen what happens when you correct or coach the hunters in your life and how their manner or attitude toward the action changes from enthusiastic to disinterested. It's not a fragile ego; it's a desire to be recognized for what they accomplish rather than what they can't or won't do.

The masculine wants to be the hero of your life. You can make them your heroes by praising their accomplishments and bragging about them to others. Looking for ways in which they are already heroes in your life is a terrific technique to make a hunter feel more masculine. Even something as small as opening a jar is an opportunity to show appreciation. When they open a jar of pickles for you, thank them. If they feel like your hero, you've got them for life. A hunter who feels appreciated will commit faster and deeper than one who doesn't.

Freedom

If you've seen the film Braveheart, you'll know that hunters require freedom. To hunt, they require the ability to go where they want, when they want. If they lose their freedom, the other party may face the wrath of a hunter who feels confined. Why do you suppose there are so many conflicts in prison? People who are currently incarcerated may feel agitated at losing their independence.

As a result, hunters require the freedom to do what they want, when they want. Really, doesn't everyone? Most people want to feel free in a relationship. Allowing them to make their own decisions without criticizing or micromanaging their every move will help them feel freer. Most likely, if they've made a poor decision, they may have already realized it and don't need someone else to point it out.

Allow them the freedom to be themselves. Because evolution is a process, their soul will develop and grow into a new person one day at a time. Most gatherers don't want a hunter who jumps when they say "jump." They want a hunter who stands by their beliefs and values, doing what he knows is best for himself and his family, not a pleaser who does what everyone wants when they want it.

If you want a hunter who is less bold, unsure, and shy, limit their freedom and independence. Controlling them will depolarize them, reduce their attraction, and drive them further away. However, the more freedom a hunter has, the more capable and well-adjusted to life they become. Control only results in a dependent person who must check in before deciding or exercising their will.

Psychological or emotional manipulation such as excuse-making, lying, exaggerating, victimizing, and yelling are other forms of control that can produce the same results as holding them back physically.[73] Does this sound healthy to you? Most likely not. So, don't control or psychologically manipulate them into doing what you want, because that will not increase passion or commitment to you or them.

Controlling a hunter is the opposite of giving him freedom. The feminine is one who yields, surrenders, and allows. This does not imply being a doormat all the time. Instead, it implies giving the hunter the final say in a decision. By allowing the hunter to choose between saying yes or no, it gives them the chance to provide and protect. If gatherers are used to controlling things, giving the hunter the final decision-making power may make the gatherer feel uneasy at first. But with time and the gatherer's commitment to giving the hunter the final verdict, the hunter can enjoy their newfound freedom to provide and make sure the gatherer gets to relax in their feminine.

To give a hunter the final verdict requires a huge amount of trust and acceptance. Can you blame a gatherer for requiring trust in order to give the hunter the freedom to have the final say in things? If the gatherer doesn't trust him, they can't accept that the hunter won't mess up, get hurt, or kill them both.

If you do not trust your partner to give you the final verdict right now, then start small. Ask your partner for their honest opinion. Acknowledge their answer and share with them your opinion. Let them process both and ask them, "If you had to decide after hearing both sides, what would it be?" Through time, you can learn that their answers are trustworthy and that they will take you into consideration. Slowly, give them their power back by giving them the freedom to choose what is best for themselves and their partners without controlling, manipulating, or taking over for them.

Also, to "give a hunter freedom" means giving them the space to just be and to let them focus on their mission or task at hand. This requires giving them "transition time."[74] This is a term coined by Alison Armstrong. Transition time is the time it takes for anyone in hunting mode to transition from one location or task to another. They need the space to put their tools down and clean up the blood, sweat, and tears of the day. In today's day and age, most men's daily war looks like an office building, construction site, or field, but it still deserves the same treatment because hunters adapted for life out in the wild.

How does this look in practice? If they are just coming home, say hi, give them a hug, and/or kiss them, then go away. It's only for a bit. Give them however much time they need so that they can put their tools down, wash off, and change their clothes.

Gatherers might want to share their day when they come home, but that can wait. It will give them time to be present and fully listen once they transition. If they are in the middle of a task, then simply ask when they can talk or help. This gives them the space to transition or prepare mentally for a later talk or activity. Many gatherers wonder why hunters aren't paying attention to them. It's not because they don't love you or care; it's because they need transition time before they can fully pay attention and focus on you.

Openness

The masculine within us all needs the feminine to open up to it. Closing off the masculine is like barring them from entering the house. They may show up, but they will not stay. As a result, it is vital that the feminine not block off the masculine. What does this look like? Be receptive, allowing, and accepting of whatever it is they are giving you, whether it be an idea, a gift, or feelings they need to share. Opening up to the masculine might be difficult for a gatherer who is not used to doing so (because of prior traumas). However, if you want the hunter to be their best selves, they need you to be open to them in body, mind, and spirit.

If the masculine gets what they want (like we talked about in earlier chapters) and need (as described in this chapter), they are more likely to commit. Who wouldn't want more of the people and things that give them what they want and need? That's how you gain a raving fan for life. Better yet, that's how you stay Soulmates.

Journal Prompts

- When was the last time you felt appreciated for what you did and who you are to your partner?
- When was the last time you appreciated someone with more than just a mere "thanks"?
- How would your partnership be right now if you appreciated each other more?
- Are you free to do what you want and be who you want daily?
- If not, does your partner often control you or stop you from doing or acting?

- What would your partnership be like if you both were free to do what you want and be who you want?
- What would it be like if you both trusted and accepted each other enough to be you and do you?
- Do you feel like your partner is open to you?
- Have you been more open or closed off with your partner?
- What would your partner be like if you were to open up to them?
- What would you be like if your partner was more open with you about everything?

What the Feminine (a.k.a. Gatherer) Needs to Commit

Based on the role they have played for much of their existence, the feminine also has specific needs. To bring out the best in gatherers, they need to feel:

- Safe
- Understood
- Seen

There is no magic amount or number of hours for each need because everyone is unique and requires various degrees of each to feel feminine.

Safety

Above all, a gatherer must be able to relax into their feminine. Their inner feminine essence cannot flow unless they feel safe. This is only possible if they feel protected at their center. Feeling unsafe is suffocating for the feminine gatherers because it keeps them from shining as brightly as they naturally do.

For feminine energy in general, what makes them feel safe varies, but what most have in common is that when hunters are more decisive and reliable, they feel safer. They can rely on their providers and protectors to take control so they don't have to. When gatherers are forced to decide, their hunting mode kicks in. This prevents them from flourishing in the way they can when they feel safe in their feminine. When a gatherer is controlling, it is a sign that they are not feeling safe and need to do whatever offers them certainty, so they call in their masculine energy instead. There is nothing wrong with this. However, it does not mean it is natural or preferred by people who feel more feminine-based.

For a variety of reasons, many gatherers become more masculine or hunter-like out of necessity. This can include their hunters not stepping up or losing their hunter (from a breakup, death, or divorce). Many single mothers get used to being the provider and protector of their kids after they divorce or their man leaves them with the kids. It often becomes difficult for single moms to adjust to a less-hunter role with another hunter who isn't the kids' father until years into the relationship. This can cause issues in the dynamics of who is in charge, and it may take time for the single mom to call in her inner gatherer again.

Someone with a feminine essence can also become more masculine if someone hurts them beforehand, so they take on the hunter role to cope with the situation and/or protect themselves. Many times, people who get hurt in traumatic ways can continue in a wounded masculine state for the rest of their lives. However, if they meet a hunter who makes them feel safe, they may be able to rest and receive their own femininity over time and give up the need to protect themselves.

Another way for gatherers to feel safe is to feel protected. Most gatherers will feel secure knowing that their stronger hunters are watching out for them. Many gatherers like it when their providers and protectors accompany them to their front door, call to check that they have arrived home, or open the door for them. This increases their feeling of safety because a larger, stronger hunter is more likely to protect them if they are nearby, aware of where they are, or on the phone with them.

Commitment also makes gatherers feel safe. Females (with wombs) are the childbearers who will carry the baby for nine months, and males are the seedbearers who can leave whenever they choose. Thus, it can make a woman feel more secure when someone feels loyal to her. Devotion ensures that if they become pregnant, they will care for the child or children beyond the nine-month pregnancy period. For this reason, before allowing their masculine lover to impregnate them, the female is the one to safeguard that they commit their partner on some level.

They will feel uneasy and question their future together if there is no loyalty or foreseeable commitment. Most fertile females with high estrogen levels will behave differently after around nine months of dating, the average time to produce a child. They will discuss marriage, having children, moving in together, or, at the very least, getting a pet together. We have many friends who got engaged around the nine-month mark because it's biological; most gatherers require commitment to feel safe enough to have kids. So, giving your gatherer more commitment will help them feel safe, and if they feel safe, they are more likely to commit to you. It's a win-win!

Understood

Back in hunter-gatherer days, the gatherer had to gather herbs and berries through the forests and meadows. As they walked, they made sure that other gatherers were nearby and spoke loudly enough to scare off any dangerous predators that were around. They also had to convey critical information such as where to find the berries, which ones were dangerous, and when to eat them. Gatherers could kill the entire tribe if someone didn't understand them and picked up the wrong berries. The desire to share is a biological drive that forces them to deliver the information as soon and with as much detail as possible. That way, their tribe, family, and hunters don't die. To listen to them was to ensure survival. Alison Armstrong calls these "meadow reports" or "berry repo rts."[2]

The most crucial thing for the feminine, though, is to be understood rather than just heard, which requires presence and awareness. Have you ever spoken to someone who was staring at you and then asked them what you said, only to find out they did not know? Because they were not present with you, they were hearing but not listening or understanding. To open up the feminine, the masculine must be present with them and listen with the intent to understand, not just to respond.

Many hunters make the mistake of trying to fix or find a solution for their gatherers rather than listening. This doesn't make the feminine feel understood because all they want is someone to "hold the bucket." They want to let out whatever they have to share (because sharing is a biological need, not a desire). Don't repair or solve their situation; instead, let them say whatever they need to say and "hold the bucket" for the gatherer until it's empty, all the while remaining present with them.

The feminine is known for its free-flowing radiance, so the more they have to close off, the less they show their true essence. For the feminine to share with someone, they need to trust them. Trust and acceptance are required for intimacy to take place, and intimacy is how they can open up. You can use the tips from the chapter on affection and intimacy to help them trust you so that they can open up.

Most feminine gatherers are more emotional, whereas the masculine leans more rationally. When listening with the intent to understand, it is important not to say they're wrong for what they feel. Emotions are not bad; no one's emotions are wrong. If you can listen without needing to fix them or tune them out, they will soon melt in your arms and open up even more since you have understood your feminine gatherer.

Seen

When walking through the meadows, gatherers must make sure the hunters see them in case a predator tries to attack and eat them. If a lion attacked them, they could die and stop bearing children if no one noticed. They had to be seen to stay alive, so gatherers need to be seen.

For gatherers to be seen by their hunters, the hunters must be present and aware of them. When a hunter is present, they will notice things that would typically go unseen. Things such as a new pair of earrings, a new hairstyle, or even a little pep in her step. When you recognize the feminine and give them genuine compliments on what you notice, they light up because they feel valued. As David Deida wrote in his book, *The Way of the Superior Man*, "Praise is literal food for feminine qualities. If you want your [gatherer] to grow in her radiance, health, happiness, love, beauty, power, and depth, praise these qualities."[75]

Noticing the feminine does not have to mean looking at something physically different about them. Perhaps they are singing, and you note how joyful they appear. When you share with her how much you love their singing, they will feel seen and appreciated. The greatest way to show gatherers that they are seen is to love them as they are, beyond the times they are all dressed up. See them for their natural beauty, personality, vitality, and spirit, for these are the elements that make up the gatherer. They will feel more like themselves, which will polarize them into a more feminine person, resulting in more attraction between the two of you.

When you give the feminine what they need, they will naturally want to commit to you. The masculine is the same. Because no one is perfect, you may not always be able or want to give them what they require, but as long as you do your best, you can both commit to each other in the long run.

Journal Prompts

- When was the last time you felt unsafe, even for a split second? A year, month, or day ago?
- When do you feel unsafe, if at all?
- When do you feel most safe around your partner?
- Can you listen to your partner without the need to solve their problem?
- Do you feel like your partner understands you most of the time and "gets" you?
- When was the last time you praised your partner? When was the last time your partner praised you?

- Do you feel seen by your partner? Do you notice your partner and any changes they make (no matter how small)?
- Have you felt seen, heard, and understood by your partner in the last week?

Committing to Each Other's Needs, Values, and Goals

When two people are carrying a load, it's lighter, right? When two people are pursuing a goal, it happens faster, yes? Then, it's important to know how to support each other in attaining the things you want and need in life. We recommend you check in with your partner and co-create your relationship's needs, values, and goals. This will allow you to work toward a common goal you can both commit to, rather than toward what each of you thinks the other person wants. That way, you can determine if the two of you can create it together.

The next set of questions will walk you through each process. Have your separate needs, values, and goals lists from Chapter 2 in hand. Each of you can bring what is important to you and interweave it together to create a beautiful masterpiece.

JOURNAL PROMPTS

- Look at your partner's needs from Chapter 2. Are you committed to helping them meet their needs, if so, how?
- Look at your partner's values from Chapter 2. Are you committed to helping them meet their values? If so, how?
- Where do your values both intertwine?
- If you shared 5 relationship values, what would they be?
- What are the common goals you two share for your lives together?
- How will you work together to meet these goals?

Now that you have committed to each other (and to each other's needs, values, and goals), you now have a safe space for relating, sharing, and being together. However, there will be times when a fight happens, no matter how committed you are. For that reason, in the next chapter, we will talk about how to resolve fights and even how to avoid them. So follow us to Chapter 8!

Chapter 8

How to Avoid and Resolve Fights

Regardless of how passionate, committed, or intimate you are, arguments, disputes, and fights will occur. Couples argue mainly about children, finances, and sex, but it can also be about something as trivial as leaving a plate in the sink. Instead of assuming arguments will never happen, let's discuss how to avoid them and how to deal with them when they do.

Why do we clash in the first place? We bicker because we disagree. Of course, you already knew that! So, what do people disagree about? We only ever disagree on a few fundamental issues, which include our wants, desires, goals, values, beliefs, rules, feelings, perceptions, and opinions. Those little things! Big fights, however, can happen when we sense any of our core beliefs or needs are in jeopardy.

This will be easy to explain, because you now know yourself better than ever thanks to Chapter 2. Does it make sense why we asked you earlier to put down most of the information about yourself and your partner? When you know what you need, value, desire, and believe in life and relationships, the "why" behind your disagreements will become clear. You will no longer have to say things like, "I do not know why we're fighting."

Rename Your Fights

The first step to avoiding a fight is to reframe it by using different words to describe it. We can avoid arguments by changing our underlying perceptions about them and changing the word argument itself to something less provoking. You can reduce the power of your arguments, disagreements, and clashes by eliminating those words from your vocabulary. Replace them with a phrase that softens the blow and reminds you of your intent: to connect.

Within our relationship, we refer to our disagreements, debates, and misunderstandings as "connected conversation." This term helps us to express ourselves without fear of being judged, since we know the other person is on our side. Use that phrase or make up your own.

Using a line like, "Let's not argue; let's have a connected conversation instead," so you and your partner can pause and begin again, recalling what you've learned in this book.

Also, a sense of humor or lightness can help to ease the sting. A *silly squabble*, *pickled pepper*, *tickled talk*, *heated hippo*, *pesky pooper*, *etc.* are all examples of this. When compared to words like fight, confrontations, battles, conflicts, feuds, or altercations, they carry a lot less weight. "We are arguing" carries far more baggage than "we are having a tickled talk." You can use any of these softeners or make up your own. Just be sure to name your conflicts something amusing or something that will break your pattern (also known as a pattern interrupt, which we will talk about later). It is an effective way to soften and reduce tension.

Journal Prompts

- What will you be renaming your fights to?
- What humorous phrase will you use to soften the fight?

Creating Safe Space

The second step towards avoiding *silly squabbles* is to create a safe space for each other to discuss *before* the connected conversation begins. Merriam-Webster defines the term "safe space" as "a place intended to be free of bias, conflict, criticism, or potentially threatening actions, ideas, or conversations."[76] It is helpful to create the conditions of a safe space for healthy communication to grow as soon as possible.

The longer you've been together, the more likely it is that things have gotten habitual, and you may have unconscious ways of approaching issues. However, if you want to transform your love, we must break the patterns by introducing some fresh approaches to dealing with your inevitable conflicts.

Setting Up Guidelines

Instead of hoping that your communication skills will get better on their own without you doing anything, try creating an environment where good communication comes naturally.

In our partnership, we call these the "C.C.C. s," or "Compassionate Communication Customs." These are particular standards that we would follow when talking with one another. We had been yelled at, blamed, given demeaning names, and more in our previous relationships, and we didn't want to bring that baggage into this partnership.

As a result, one day we sat down and made a set of criteria for how we wanted to communicate with each other. This list (shown below) has helped us to feel less pain and trauma, as well as reduced the number of *tickled talks* we have. By making this list and sticking to it with love, we have been able to lessen and bring more compassion into our *pickled peppers* while making them less frequent.

Below is a list of our Compassionate Communication Customs. We did not create this in one shot. Rather, we built on it over time, adding to it as we went about our lives. Whenever we were in a *heated hippo* and one or both of us did something we didn't like, we would add it to our list.

Our Compassionate Communication Customs

- No yelling
- No blaming
- No finger pointing
- No degrading language
- We each take turns speaking
- No talk of divorce or break up
- No blackmailing or demanding

- No use of force or violent language
- No going cold and numbing yourself
- No walking away unless we both agree
- Remember, we are partners and teammates
- Keep an open body posture to stay open minded
- No talk about the past—only present tense and future talk
- Avoid exaggerating or using words like "always" and "never"
- No closed-off body language (crossing of hands, arms, legs, etc.)
- We are on the same side and both want to make each other happy
- Listen intently from a place to understand and not to just respond
- Play peaceful music in the background (such as binaural beats)

You are free to use all, some, or none of these, or to construct your own based on your requirements and ideals. It is up to you what to include in your list of customs or guidelines, and you can name them whatever you want. The goal here is for both of you to have a say in what goes on your list. Construct them together by thinking of and feeling empathy for each other.

Journal Prompts

- If you had it all your way, how would all conversations between you and your partner go?
- What are some things you never want to happen during a discussion together?
- What are some ways of communicating that you would like to instill in your conversations?
- What is your relationship list of customs or guidelines for your connected conversations or tickled talks?

Create Designated Times to Talk

Many couples are so caught up in their daily activities, they forget to spend quality, undistracted time together. This is especially crucial for the feminine, since when the masculine is present and listening, they feel heard and understood. So, make time in your schedule to communicate about your day, what you learned, what you encountered, and what you are feeling or thinking.

We like to do this while eating because it doesn't take much time out of our day and there's no reason not to since we both have to eat. So, instead of watching TV or scrolling through social media, we set aside this time for each other. We each get 15 minutes to speak about anything we choose, without interruption (apart from "yeses," "aha's," and so on) and without limitations. This gives us each 15 minutes to explain what's going on.

We've also discovered that scheduling a once-a-week date night with quality time and a review conversation really connects us together. The weekly review provides a recap of the previous week's events. Miscommunication or a lack of communication is one reason people argue. If you don't communicate about something, for example, like your partner leaving the toilet paper roll empty, you may blow up and start an argument after a tough day at work. This can leave them confused and at a loss for what's really going on. You can prevent all of this by making time to discuss the previous week and using the four-step framework for conflict resolution (found after the upcoming journal prompts).

Journal Prompts

- When can you and your partner create time each day for each other?
- Which day and time would be best for your weekly

review?

- During your daily talks, how much time will you each give yourself to speak without interruption?
- During your talks, what are some things you would like to go over?

Four-Step Framework for Resolving Fights

After adding more affection, passion, and commitment, there will be a brief period when everything is bright and lovely again. However, eventually there might be difficulties. Those issues can result in less-than-pleasant "discussions" with your partner. Let's be honest: you're going to fight, it's inevitable, unless you are robots who never speak to one another (which is a whole other problem).

Do your best to reconcile these disagreements because, according to epidemiological data compiled by a team of psychiatric researchers, marital conflict is a risk factor for sickness and mortality.[77] Fighting in a relationship has the potential to kill you, literally. So, how do you cope with the inevitable fights that will arise? Buckle (or B.U.C.L.) your seatbelt; we're going on a ride!

We employ a four-step approach to resolve conflicts:

1. **Be in Service**: Commit to putting your relationship and partner first.

2. **Understand**: Know the reason for the fight.

3. **Compromise**: Find a solution that meets both of your needs.

4. **Love**: Give your partner unconditional love.

Serving your partner is a state of putting them first, which opens the door to understanding and offers clarity about what's wrong. Once you have that foundation, you can reach a compromise that is best for both of you and then love them unconditionally, regardless of the outcome.

Step 1: Be in Service

The first step toward preventing another fight is to serve, and we're not talking IRS-style serving. This means serving your partner and your relationship. This is not just an external activity but a mental condition in which you decide to prioritize your partner and your relationship.

As covered in Chapter 1, we all have a choice in every situation: to serve others or to serve ourselves. Our relationship operates the same way as a battery: there is a negative (which is taking energy) and a positive (which is giving energy). Sometimes you can either take or give.

Yes, sometimes you must serve yourself because you need to eat and drink, for example. However, if you want your relationship to grow, you must each give more than you take.

The willingness to serve your partner or yourself can mean the difference between wanting to resolve a conflict or not. If you're in a taking mode, you're preoccupied with yourself, so resolving the argument isn't a higher priority than watching TV or entertaining yourself. If you choose to serve your partner (and the relationship), you are more likely to want to work things out rather than ignore them. Of course, if you are going to die of thirst, you must take a sip of water (which is serving yourself). In this case, we're talking about a willingness to serve your mate and your relationship most of the time, even during a conflict.

When you are in a state of service, you want to give to your significant other, which means giving them your energy, attention, and love above all else. This is the first step because you cannot understand or compromise unless you are willing to serve your partner. The framework's second and third steps are impossible to complete without a willingness to give to your partnership. So, even though this step is more of a mental state than an action, it is necessary before moving on to step 2, which is to understand.

More than anything, being of service is a state of mind and a way of being. You are more likely to act lovingly in this state of mind because you are coming from a place of service to the relationship and your partner. As a result, even if they provoked you, you're more inclined to be gracious about any wrongdoing they may have committed. There will be times when this seems impossible because they did something that seems beyond repair. However, we never said serving others before yourself would be easy. Serving them, even when they have done something horrible, is the ultimate sign of humility, love, and service. If you need time to come from a place of service, then take all the time you need and come back to love once the steam has cooled off.

Step 2: Understand

The second step is to know what you're fighting about and why you're fighting. If you don't know why you started arguing, it might escalate into a more intense debate. To do this, you need to know yourself, your needs, beliefs, values, rules, etc., before you can understand your partner. It sounds like Chapters 2 and 3, doesn't it? Did it have to do with your needs, values, beliefs, rules, or traumas, which are the parts of you that developed early in life and are more hardwired? Or was it more about your desires, goals, feelings, opinions, or perceptions, which are more malleable because they change from minute to minute?

Our needs, values, beliefs, and rules get established when we are young, so they are more a part of who we are. Even though they can change, they tend to stay the same for most of our lives unless we choose to change them. Our goals, feelings, opinions, and perceptions can change from moment to moment based on the day and the situation. When you argue, you need to figure out if you disagree about things that are hard-wired and deeply seated or things that aren't.

In every situation, it's important to know what your partner needs because that's the starting point for everything. If your partner is hungry and you just want to connect with them, an argument might happen because they are more interested in food (a.k.a. certainty) and talking to you is distracting them from getting their basic needs met. But until you know what you both need, the argument may seem useless. So, it's important to first understand what they need and then dig deeper to see if other parts of them (or you) are causing the conflict.

The easiest way to figure out who felt offended is to determine who started the fight. For example, you may have a rule that says you work for an hour every morning on your most important task to feel accomplished. So, you get to your computer to start on that task when your loved one interrupts by putting one of your talkative uncles on the phone without checking in. The call takes up your entire morning, so you don't have time to work on your task. You might get angry and start a fight about what happened. Since your rule was broken, it's clear that you were the one who started the argument. To stop this from happening again, you and your partner need to understand this rule.

Let's take your needs as an example because they are the most fundamental aspect of what makes you unique. Imagine you want certainty while your partner wants a lot more uncertainty. What do you think happens when you take a vacation or travel? You need safety and security, so you spend hours planning and preparing, whereas your partner looks for adventure and believes that preparation ruins the sense of adventure. An argument might ensue on how to go about the vacation. When we apply our understanding to this, we can see that if everyone knows what they need, it is easier to figure out what the dispute is about. From there, you can decide to serve your partner and prioritize their needs, and then you can reach a compromise that works for the relationship. By finding a compromise that works for the relationship, you are not just avoiding a "pickled pepper" this time, you are creating a solution to avoid all future "pickled peppers." This can resolve arguments about anything, including your values, beliefs, and rules.

Let's look at how this can apply to your soft-wired elements, such as your feelings, beliefs, and opinions. These can shift from moment to moment, so when you have a feeling or opinion about something, you must first understand yourself. Where is this feeling, belief, or opinion coming from? Is it tied to a need, value, or rule? Once you understand yourself, you can grasp the needs of your partner. When you establish this, you can consider compromising. The same is true for your opinions and perceptions about anything, because while they may alter, it's still important to understand each other before moving on to the next level.

True understanding comes from listening with the desire to understand rather than respond. We're often so focused on getting a word in that we neglect to listen to what the other person is saying. Many clashes result in couples just trading words while no one is listening, so they end up running in circles rather than reaching a solution. So, before we can agree, we must first grasp what our partner is saying, needing, feeling, and so on.

Knowing not just what the other person is thinking but also what they are experiencing leads to a deeper understanding. This also requires a level of awareness that extends beyond the logical mind and delves into the emotional depth of what your companion is feeling during the conflict. Here's when empathy comes in handy. You can discern what they are thinking, but that seldom results in the type of resolution that makes a person say, "They get me." It just requires a willingness to listen with the intent to understand what your partner is feeling by putting yourself in their shoes, so to speak.

When you empathize with another person, you share their feelings. This level of comprehension causes you to see things through their eyes and feel their emotions. True empathy comes from being open and sensitive to the other person; hence, it will be impossible to empathize if you're closed off or rigid in your viewpoint. This might be tough for people to change, so it may take some practice. However, it is possible to soften and open up if you will share your own emotions and sentiments. Empathy is one of those things that cannot happen unless you are prepared to go there with your partner.

Once you understand them and what is causing the conflict, you can solve the problem with Step 3, which is to compromise.

Step 3: Compromise

Once you have served your partner and understood them and the reason behind the fight, you can work on agreeing. The point of this compromise is to create a win-win situation for both of you. Life is too short to waste time in a relationship where one or both people are losing. This agreement has to work for them as much as it does for you. If it doesn't serve you both, then it wouldn't serve the relationship either.

Compromise requires each side to make concessions (to concede or surrender). Since both of you are coming from a state of service and understanding, this makes it much easier to concede or grant something to them. This doesn't mean letting your partner walk all over you; it means yielding to each other and laying down your weapons.

Communicating with vulnerability is a great way to yield and get your partner to do the same. Vulnerability means being exposed, open, and able to be attacked, but still showing up. When we are vulnerable, we are more honest and real, which builds trust with others and encourages others to be vulnerable as well. The opposite is also true. If we close ourselves off, other people will do the same to protect themselves.

The alternative to giving in is to yell at each other, puff out your chest, and try to "win" by getting the upper hand in the argument. But when one person wins, the other person loses in this scenario. Instead, we want to find a solution that works for both sides. This happens when you first "bow" to each other, then put down your swords and work together to fix the problem. Once you both yield and stop the desire to "win" the argument, you can think win-win to come up with a solution that works for everyone. This is a true compromise. The point isn't to avoid conflict but to stop wanting to beat the other person or win, because your relationship is not a battle.

You can leave the argument if you need time to figure out how to solve things on your own. With time, you can talk to your partner about your ideas for resolving the problem. If you're the person who avoids conflict or who feels trapped and blows up when you're in a tight spot, then take a quick break from the situation. One of our favorite ways to figure out when we need to step away is to use "safe words." We say things like "buttermilk pancakes" because it's an inside joke between us. This has made one or both of us laugh enough to stop our ears from steaming. So, use a safe word if you need a moment to calm down, and try to find one that makes you both laugh or smile.

Compromising with Requests vs. Demands

Most people find it hard to compromise because they end up being too demanding. A demand makes the other person back away or do the opposite. There is a fine line between asking for something and demanding it. In his book, *Nonviolent Communication*, Marshall Rosenberg talks about the difference between a request and a dem and.[78] We will take his approach to compromise in this step, so that you both get what you want without making demands that upset the other person.

According to the Britannica Dictionary, a request means "to ask for [something] in a polite or formal way."[79] Demand means "to say in a forceful way that something must be done or given to you."[80] One can refuse a request because it is not a demand. If you are serving your partner and the relationship, it is not mandatory for your partner to comply with your request. Demanding makes you more like a dictator than a lover.

You may believe you are making a request, but your tone or manner of asking makes it appear to be a demand. We can see the difference between the two in how we ask, because to demand is to ask with authority, but to request is to ask with politeness. If you try to compromise with your partner by raising your voice or asking with authority, this is a demand, not a request. What do you believe their likely response to this demand would be? The idea is to reach a compromise that benefits both of you. If you are demanding, it won't lead to a win-win situation; someone is already losing because of the way you are asking.

Another way to tell if you are requesting or demanding is to watch how you react to their response. Let's say they say no to your request. If the way you deal with it is to criticize, blame, or act rejected, then it was a demand, not a request. If you want to achieve a win-win situation, you must request, not demand, and be willing for them to say no, using understanding and empathy.

Let's take the following example: Imagine your partner desires a foot massage. The manner in which they choose to inform you is, "Where is my massage? It's been a long time. I'm entitled to one." What is your automatic reaction? Even if you wanted to offer them a foot rub before, you won't now. If your primary response is to oppose or submit, this tells you it was a demand rather than a request because they didn't consider your decision or free will. As a result, you decline the "request," and they become enraged and lash out at you for not giving them a foot rub. You now have proof that it was a demand rather than a request. Does that make you want to massage them in the future? Most likely not.

When someone demands something, they believe they deserve the thing or action they are demanding. Underneath is an unnoticed need. If we are to compromise, we must first become conscious of our own demands. We need to identify our own needs before we try to pass them on in an impolite manner as a demand (which may not be intentional).

So, before you share your truth in a nasty way, delve a little deeper. Ask yourself, "What do I *need*?" That way, you can request it from them. However, keep in mind that a request implies that someone may say no. Be prepared for your request to be declined, or else you are being demanding, and we all know how that ends.

Journal Prompts

- Has your partner demanded something in the last week?
- Have you demanded something from your partner in the last week?
- How will you turn a demand into a request from now on?

Step 4: Love

"The way of the miracle-worker is to see all human behavior as one of two things: either love, or a call for love."[81]- Marianne Williamson

The final stage in this process is to love them unconditionally. Love without conditions or constraints is love without boundaries or restraints. It is more about the verb "love" than the noun. The act of showing love while feeling it in your heart is what this phase is all about. It's as easy as hugging, kissing, tickling, telling your partner how much you love them, or having pillow wars with laughter and joy. You now know what their love language is, so express your love in their language. If they aren't good with words but enjoy receiving things, a hug might not be as useful to them as a gift.

It is important that no matter what agreements you reach, you conclude any fights with love. Even after you've reached a compromise, there may be leftover bitterness or animosity from comments made before you made concessions. This can leave a nasty taste in your mouth, especially if it was full of emotion and you or your partner said things that cannot be unsaid. Isn't when you're upset (like after a silly squabble) the time that you need love the most? When you love unconditionally, you create a positive emotional state for your partner, letting them know that no matter what happens, you still care for them.

Another great way to show love is to look them in the eyes and apologize for anything you said or did. This may be challenging for folks battling with pride or thinking, "They started it" or "I did nothing wrong." That may be true, but these thoughts will not grow your relationship or show love. So, in this scenario, say you're sorry, and the chances of them expressing the same increase. We almost always stop our arguments swiftly because we apologize, even if neither of us has anything to apologize for. This act of love is enough to make the other person reassess their feelings and respond in a more loving manner.

If you have nothing to apologize for, say sorry for getting mad (if you did) and not displaying love throughout the entire fight. Your anger may be justified, but that is not the point here. The idea is to love, and love has no boundaries or limits. So, if you want to fix things, demonstrate love, even if that means apologizing when you don't have to.

Show them unconditional love with no restrictions or feelings other than love, joy, and peace. Watch how quickly they melt in your arms, as if everything is fine in the world. The goal of your union was to unite and grow further in love, right? So, why not end all disputes with the love you want?

Journal Prompts

- How can you practice giving your partner love unconditionally, even after a quarrel?
- How can you practice saying sorry after every argument or fight, even if it's not your fault?
- How can you give them love using their love language, even after a disagreement?

Breaking Their Pattern

If your partner refuses to come from a place of service to understand, compromise, and love, then break their pattern. Pattern breaking is a technique used in neuro-linguistic programming (NLP) that helps people get rid of bad habits and feelings by breaking the daily patterns they have learned. It can also avoid the arguments altogether because it will break their state or interrupt the pattern that is about to cause a scuffle.

This works because humans become trapped in unconscious vicious circles (also known as subconscious negative patterns) that place them in the same unproductive emotional states. If we can interrupt those patterns before they begin or while they are happening, we can shift the person's state and make them more receptive to resolving the issue together.

State Breaks

The first method for breaking someone's pattern is a state break. In a nutshell, it breaks their state, thus the name! You do so by asking them random, unrelated questions to get them out of their unresourceful emotional state. Our minds need to answer questions, no matter what they are or when they occur. So, if you're arguing with your lover and you randomly ask them if they're hungry, they'll have to react, whether in their heads or out loud. You can go back to the conversation like normal after that. However, if they go back into that same emotional state, then you can pose another unconnected and random inquiry to "break" it. The point is to break their state by asking questions to get them away from those feelings of anger, frustration, or other non-loving emotions.

For example, if you and your partner are fighting over dirty dishes, you might ask them, "Do you think I should clean these before or after we talk?" This can cause a total halt to the previous argument, at which point it may resume or stop for enough time to cool off. The point is to avoid an undesirable emotional state. If the pattern returns, repeat. It's never too late to break their state, so if it happens, rinse and repeat, and eventually it will never return in the same way, again.

Pattern Interrupts

Pattern interrupts are the second approach for disrupting someone's pattern. According to clinical hypnotist and NLP trainer Lee S. Avery, "State Breaks are... designed to pull a client out of a single emotional position." He says, "Pattern interrupts are more sophisticated [than state breaks] since they must break the client out of a long-standing behavior pattern."[82] Our patterns are so ingrained and subconscious at this stage that you must do something wild and expressive to break them out of their regular inclination. We've heard of people tickling or kissing their partners. Be as outrageous, fun, and outlandish as the circumstance requires. Just be cautious if there is anything that could further irritate your partner, such as extreme noises, which could stir up a childhood trauma.

The more random and comical your pattern interrupt, the more likely it is to do its job. We have a pattern interrupt where one of us says "BOO!" when we become tired or the other person says something like, "I'm tired." This is outrageous, yet it works. Sometimes, you have to go far out of the norm to get a response that breaks their pattern.

Another way to break their pattern is by making a random sound, such as an exaggerated sneeze (even if it's fake), that can catch their attention. If you can manage it, farting is also a nice one (because it's funny in a tense situation). You can also play sound effects from your phone to lighten the mood and interrupt their pattern. Be mindful that the other party usually wants to return to their undesirable state, but you may perform another pattern interrupt again and again. After a while, they are likely to be unable to return to that pattern in that way, so you have a better foundation from which to resolve the issue.

Breaking someone's pattern is especially helpful if you set them off or touched a trauma wound that hasn't fully healed. While it is not your responsibility to cure their trauma, you may help them remove the anchors that produced the trauma. Eventually, the strong feelings may lose their potency, and the associated feelings can diminish.

If you did something that brought the trauma to the surface, you can apply the following approach: Let's imagine you hurt your partner with something you said. So, every time they talk about it, they fall into the same pattern of looking down and crying. Instead of allowing this to happen again, startle your partner by pretending you saw a spider. This will surprise them and get them out of their trance. They may return to that pattern, but this time you can pose a question that distracts their attention, such as, "Oh my God, did I leave the stove on again? Let me double-check!" Then return and repeat if they enter that state again. If you interrupt the pattern enough times, they cannot return to that state in the same way with the same emotions.

Knowing Each Other's Trauma Responses

Have you ever felt like you're no longer fully present but are somewhere in a past traumatic event? Maybe you find yourself locked in by a jammed door, and you start to feel a panic attack starting. Maybe you were near a shooting, and the sound of loud bangs now terrifies you. Whatever the case, these incidents, whether small or large, can play a role in how we react to certain situations in the present moment.

Knowing what trauma responses your partner might have from the past is useful information if you'd like to avoid disputes. We want to take this a step further and reveal our dislikes and pet peeves. Since they'll come up anyhow, we might as well be aware of them.

If you know what brings up strong negative emotions for you, then share this with your partner. Then, they can do their best to avoid these things around you. If you do not know what provokes you right away, then it may be a good idea for you to create a list of things you love and things that you hate (the opposite of what you love). For example, "I despise clutter and adore cleanliness." See how this would influence your partner to organize more? Consider spending years doing things for your partner that you believe they enjoy, but they secretly despise them. This can lead to silent resentment. With these insights, you can understand more about yourself and them.

You'll also want them to be aware of things that cause you stress, such as leaving the door unlocked or forgetting to close it. If they're not aware of your quirks, this can lead to issues. A stranger may have entered the house when you were a child, so you now keep all doors secured. Knowing why the situation causes a cascade of strong emotions is less crucial in this case than knowing what they are, because we aren't attempting to trace back every trauma to its source; we want to be aware of what they are so our partner can help us avoid doing them from a place of love. Although, if you know the "why" behind the traumatic response and write it down, your partner may have more empathy and a better understanding of how important it is to you. They will be more likely to remember and avoid it.

Fear, anger, and yelling are attempts to avoid pain and a cry for love. Knowing what pain your partner is avoiding can help you understand the problem. Instead of attacking each other, you're now working together to understand the deeper meaning. When you discover the deeper meaning behind their cries for love, be on their side to create a win-win that will avoid their pain, pet peeves, and traumas.

If you can avoid activating negative traumatic responses in your partner, you are less likely to have fights, especially when you know what they really want and need, which this book has shown you.

Your goal now is to jot down the things that bother you so they can stop irritating you! It's time to share everything you detest! Make a list of the things, people, or circumstances that aggravate you.

Journal Prompts

- What makes you tick?
- What frustrates, annoys, or bothers you?
- What should I avoid doing while we are together?
- What are you most scared of?
- What are some things your parents did that you don't want me to do?
- What are some things your previous partners did that you don't want me to do?

∞

Your Last Big Supportive Step

Share the secrets of keeping intimacy, passion, and commitment alive in a relationship.

You now know how to cultivate intimacy, enhance passion, strengthen commitment, and improve communication while resolving conflict with your partner.

By leaving your honest opinion of this book on Amazon, you'll show other couples how they can enjoy an exciting, healthy, loving relationship in the long term.

You can make a difference for other couples by sharing your experience of reading this book. If you haven't already, please take a minute now to leave a review of this book on Amazon. This will encourage other readers to work on the skills they need to bring their best selves to their relationship and feel deep love with their life partner.

Thank you!

Chapter 9

Conclusion

∞

Congratulations on reaching the end of this book! As we close, let's discuss what to do next. We want your renewed relationship to last. So, we will show you how to keep this new level of intimacy, passion, and commitment despite the inevitable challenges that emerge. Obstacles will arise, and we want you to be ready for them.

Make the Choice

Let's revisit the question of who you're going to serve. Are you going to spend most of your time serving yourself? Or are you going to serve others? If you've read this far, you likely want to put them before yourself (most of the time). This doesn't mean you're a martyr or that you starve yourself. It means you serve your partner, your relationship, and others before yourself.

When you select the route of serving others first, you are taking the path of love, oneness, unity, selflessness, respect for free will, and giving to others. An example of this is someone who allows someone (who is clearly in a hurry) to cut in front of them in line even though they waited awhile. This path works *with* the universe because, as you have seen in organizations, teams, families, and relationships, when things work together, they work better. When you help, give, support, and love, you are more likely to receive the same things in return, allowing you to achieve your goals faster and with greater cohesion. As a result, this path is known as the "positive path" (a.k.a. the path of love), which leads to a harmonious union with your partner.

There is one historical character who stands out as selfless because he devoted his life to showing humankind the way of love, oneness, and forgiveness. Even on his deathbed, or death post, he begged God to forgive his persecutors because "they know not what they do." His name was Yehoshua, or Jesus.

The path of serving yourself before others is the path of hatred, ego, chaos, separation, greediness, and violating the free will of others. It is the way of power, dominance over others, control, and separation. It is also known as the "negative path." An example of this is someone who charges to the front of a line after people have been waiting for hours because they believe their own needs are more important. The Service to Self path is the path of takers and those who lie, steal, and/or cheat their way through life. Seeing as nothing in the universe functions in solitude, it is the path of entropy, disharmony, and chaos. You may succeed (in a sense) in taking this route, but you could end up alone. Will you truly be happy if you are alone forever?

A young boy named Joseph is an excellent example of this negative path. As a child, he engaged in bullying, violence, and destruction. As he became more famous and took control of the USSR in 1929, he sought greater control to satisfy his unquenchable craving for power and global dominance. Scholars estimate that, before his death, he slaughtered at least 40 million of his own people, with some estimates as high as 60 million.[83] His last name was Stalin, one of the founding fathers of communism.

Maybe you never considered this choice or didn't even know you had a choice. We all have a choice in each moment; that is what free will is about. What is important is that you make this choice with intention, because the sinkhole of indifference is where most people are. They are stuck between both polarities, not committed to serving others or themselves. It is important to know that when you serve others you serve yourself, because what goes around comes around. Make the choice and commit to putting either yourself or your partner first most of the time. The choice is yours.

Unity vs. Separation

If you've chosen the path of serving others, you've chosen oneness and harmony, which means doing everything you can to stay with your partner through thick and thin. Whatever happens, you choose love over fear, unity over division, and harmony over turmoil. If every time something horrible happens, you explode and seek to end your relationship, it's clear which path you've taken. The path of love and unity requires you to serve your partner and your relationship first by working it out, even if you'd rather serve yourself by watching TV or distracting yourself.

Choosing to make the choice every day, every hour, and especially when a challenging obstacle appears takes intention and determination. If you make a mistake and choose the negative path of separation or disharmony, forgive yourself. Then move forward by reestablishing your choice of love, unity, oneness, and harmony. Your partner and relationship will appreciate it.

Forgiveness

If you've chosen the positive road of service to others, then learn the art of forgiveness. Forgive for whatever was said or done, and begin as if you were meeting for the first time. To forgive, let go of resentments you had prior to reading this book. It's too late to change the past.

If you're reading this book, you're over the concept of breaking up or divorcing. So, it's time to forgive and move on. Forgive yourself for any actions that led to, caused, or made the problem or situation worse. Forgive your partner for the past, and remember that you are both one being in two bodies; therefore, forgiving them is also forgiving yourself. You also make mistakes and blunders, and you have suffered enough because of your trespasses. Allow them the privilege and honor of no longer feeling guilty about what they did. We would never sleep if we dwelled on every wrongdoing we committed. Allow your lover to forgive themselves, knowing they have already paid enough for their faults and now deserve peace as much as you do.

If you're having trouble forgiving your partner, do this: look in the mirror and admit you're not without blame. Everyone makes mistakes sometimes. We all likely harmed someone, in some way, or acted selfishly to someone in our life at some point. Have you not cut someone off in traffic, told a white lie, gossiped behind someone's back, or cheated on a test? Nobody is flawless, and you shouldn't expect your partner to be. So, forgive yourself and them for the past, present, and future.

Acceptance

Total acceptance is required for forgiveness. To forgive, you must accept your partner as they are, baggage and all. Accept your partner's flaws, sins, and shortcomings. They do not require constant reminders of their mistakes to progress and grow. Accepting people for who they are means accepting their past, present, and beyond.

When accepting your partner, you accept their personality and even who they were before this moment. You are also accepting their future selves without feeling the need to control their activities and behaviors. To do this, you must let go of control over their every action and respect their nature so they can live with free will. This does not mean you accept offensive behavior or abuse, because we all need boundaries at times. A simple stern look or tone of voice will work wonders to stop the bad treatment. If that doesn't work, simply taking your attention away from them will usually warn them that you are not pleased with something.

However, you have no control over how they spend their time or what they do with their lives. It is your responsibility to accept them for who they are. Accept their beliefs, values, needs, goals, opinions, viewpoints, and emotions without criticizing them. Allow them to have different ways of thinking, being, and feeling while still loving them.

Unconditional Love

The ultimate purpose of this book is love. Accepting your partner for who they are and what they do is to love them without conditions, regardless of their past, present, or future choices. Love solves everything. If you can love them at every moment, you can solve most problems.

Love them with no other goal in mind than to give them love. Love them as though they were you in a different body. Consider how much you would adore them if you had made them, just like a mother loves her baby. If you can love your partner (and everyone) that much, you will have lifelong supporters, helpers, and raving fans.

Many people only love someone with limits. In the book, *A Course in Miracles*, they refer to this as a "special relationship" because one loves only under specific condit ions.[84] For example, if they earn a particular amount of money or do certain things for you, only then will you show them love. Yet, when those conditions change, such as when they are unkind, lose their wealth, or don't do things for you, the love you offer them fades (in a special relationship.)

A "holy relationship" is what *A Course in Miracles* refers to as a relationship where one loves regardless of what other people do.[85] Even though a newborn cries and vomits all over its parents, they still adore their baby, with no difference in the amount or type of love provided. Regardless of the circumstances, adore your partner as if they were your child. Care for them even when they sulk, stomp, yell, and ignore you, because your love for them doesn't wane since your love for them is eternal, limitless, and unconditional. That is a holy relationship. That is unconditional love.

Begin loving them as much as you would love your own child. Do this through the use of baby voices and baby nicknames. For example, in our relationship, when we talk to each other (unless we're discussing business), we use voices that sound like two toddlers babbling to each other. We also assigned each other nicknames we use more often than our real names, which are Mr. and Mrs. Sweet Sweet, Baby Waby, and Baby Waby-kins (just to name a few). When we use these voices and nicknames, it encourages us to treat each other tenderly, as if each were a delicate flower we don't want to step on. As a result, the likelihood of fighting or even yelling decreases. Test it out for yourself.

Restart and Renew

What are you going to do now? We feel that after reading this book, couples should start over. Ask your partner to "start again" so you can put the past behind you and move forward with all the new knowledge you have acquired. Attempt to avoid bringing up the past by leaving it in the past. Restart your relationship with your partner.

Restart as if today were the first day you met. Start over with your relationship in peace, with complete forgiveness and acceptance of one another. Set your emotional bank account, which accumulates both happy and bad feelings over time, to zero. This means you don't bring up anything from your history that occurred before you arrived at this point. Leave it in the past and treat your partner as if they will handle things differently.

Give them (and yourself) a genuine shot at pleasure by not depriving them of the gift that everyone has—the present moment. There is no need to remind them of who they were or what they did. Begin again, be present with them, and appreciate who they are right now.

Accomplish this by renewing your vows to each other or creating new vows that leave behind the past and show what you plan to do more of in the future. An example would be, "I vow to no longer [insert old] and I vow to [insert new] from now on." For example, "I vow to no longer hold you accountable for mistakes you made in the past or will make in the future, and I vow to love you even when I am upset from now on." You can use that template or make your own. It doesn't have to be perfect as long as it is genuine. This is a fresh start from which you can build.

Journal Prompts

- If you could start over with your partner, what would you do differently?
- If you could start over with your partner, what would you say to let them know you want the best for both of you?
- What do you vow to no longer do moving forward with and for your partner?
- What do you commit to doing more of now and in the future with and for your partner?

If You're Still Struggling

If you're having trouble starting over, forgiving them, loving them, and being of service to them, there's a simple solution: imagine them gone from your life. When Tim Ferriss told the TED Talk audience to imagine the worst-case scenario rather than the best-case scenario, he was referring to a concept known as "fear setting."[86] People will go to great lengths to avoid pain, so imagine life without your partner and feel how life without them would be. Consider having no more walks, meals, and conversations with them. How does it make you feel? When we consider they could be gone tomorrow, it changes our perspective on them and makes us appreciate them more.

Take it a step further and imagine life if they were no longer alive. As morbid as it may sound, when someone dies, we erase all the flaws or mistakes they had or made. According to the list of the "Top Ten Regrets of the Dying" they wished they had spent more time with them and said "I love you" more.[87]

Another technique is to imagine today as your last day on Earth. The adage "live each day as if it were your last" may inspire you to make amends and forgive. An article on dailymail.com featured the Twitter feed of Dr.

Alastair McAlpine of Paedspal Cape Town pediatric palliative care, who asked dying children about what they enjoyed and what gave life meaning for them. None of them said they enjoyed fighting with others.[88] We believe you would feel the same way since one of the top regrets of the dying was, "I should have been the bigger person and resolved the conflict(s)."[89]

Use this method to determine whether you want to spend the rest of your life filled with rage, resentment, and hatred, or to live a life full of passion, commitment, intimacy, and love. If you choose the latter, you must forgive, forget, and move on like today is your last day. Love your partner as they are, and your relationship will grow into one in which you adore, appreciate, cherish, and care for each other as one.

The Beginning, Not The End

This may be the end of the book, but it begins your new life. You can now start over and have a relationship you want to shout about from the rooftops. Your renewed relationship will become a partnership in which you work as a team and as one unit toward your shared vision and mission as a couple.

Once you have mastered the concepts and practices in this book, you will live a life where you understand yourself and your partner better than anyone else. Understanding each other from the inside out entails knowing what the other person needs, wants, believes, and values in life. With these new insights, you will know if something is wrong, and you can pinpoint what it is. The likelihood of you being confused about what is going on is much lower since you know yourself and your partner so well.

You will have more intimacy and affection with your partner now that you know how to become best friends with them and know them on a deeper level. The more you do the journal prompts and apply the principles in this book, the more trusting and open you will be to each other. After reading this couple's guide, you should never feel as if you don't know or trust your partner.

You also understand how to add more passion to your relationship, so you still desire each other as much as when you first met. More desire means more enjoyable sex and wilder rides.

Since you have increased your commitment, the possibility of straying, cheating, or not wanting to be together decreases. Especially since you now know what level of commitment you both have, want, and are working toward together.

You can also use your own Compassion Communication Customs to avoid arguments. You can resolve conflicts if they happen by creating a safe space for communication and following our four-step process. It begins with being of service to your partner and ends with unconditional love. If one or both of you can't seem to get out of the pattern, you know how to break the cycle to get them in a better state and avoid the argument altogether.

Now you have all the tools. Go use them with your partner. Remember to serve each other and your relationship, forgive one another, accept one another, and love each other no matter what.

A Gift From Us

Seeking more information on how to deepen your relationship's intimacy, passion, and commitment? Receive a list of activities you can do together as a couple, conversation topics you can discuss, and how to add more of all the ingredients into your newfound healthy relationship. To get all the extra goodies and join our email list, go to https://www.infinitecreationsinc.com/learntol ove or scan the QR code below with your smartphone or tablet:

Please also leave a gift for others by leaving a review about your experience during and after reading this book. You can leave a review by using this link: https: //bit.ly/Review-L2L

Thank you.

1. FastStats - Marriage and Divorce. "FastStats," February 23, 2023. https://www.cdc.gov/nchs/fastats/marriage-divorce.htm.
2. Laws of Motion - Everything2.com. "Laws of Motion - Everything2.Com," n.d. https://everything2.com/title/Laws+of+Motion.
3. Maslow, A. H. "A Theory of Human Motivation." Psychological Review 50, no. 4 (July 1943): 370–96. https://doi.org/10.1037/h0054346.
4. Mcleod, Saul. "Maslow's Hierarchy of Needs." Editted by Olivia Guy-Evans. Simply Psychology, December 29, 2007. https://www.simplypsychology.org/maslow.html?Tag=schedule.
5. Owens, Alexandra. "Tell Me All I Need to Know About Oxytocin." Edited by Randy Bressler. Psycom, September 23, 2021. https://www.psycom.net/oxytocin.
6. Matsushita, Hiroaki, Hein Min Latt, Yuuri Koga, Teiichi Nishiki, and Hideki Matsui. "Oxytocin and Stress: Neural Mechanisms, Stress-Related Disorders, and Therapeutic Approaches." Neuroscience 417 (October 2019): 1–10. https://doi.org/10.1016/j.neuroscience.2019.07.046.

7. Watson, Stephanie. "Oxytocin: The Love Hormone." Harvard Health Publishing, July 20, 2021. https://www.health.harvard.edu/mind-and-mood/oxytocin-the-love-hormone.
8. Smith, J C, J A Mercy, and J M Conn. "Marital Status and the Risk of Suicide." American Journal of Public Health 78, no. 1 (January 1988): 78–80. https://doi.org/10.2105/ajph.78.1.78.
9. Positive, The Daily. "Top 10 Regrets Of The Dying." The Daily Positive, July 18, 2014. https://www.thedailypositive.com/top-10-regrets-dying/.
10. Harvard Study. "Harvard Second Generation Grant and Glueck Study," n.d. https://www.adultdevelopmentstudy.org/grantandglueckstudy.
11. Waldinger, Robert. "What Makes a Good Life? Lessons from the Longest Study on Happiness." Robert Waldinger: What makes a good life? Lessons from the longest study on happiness | TED Talk, n.d. https://www.ted.com/talks/robert_waldinger_what_makes_a_good_life_lessons_from_the_longest_study_on_happiness/c.
12. Braithwaite, Scott, and Julianne Holt-Lunstad. "Romantic Relationships and Mental Health." Current Opinion in Psychology 13 (February 2017): 120–25. https://doi.org/10.1016/j.copsyc.2016.04.001.

13. Stokes, Jeffrey E., and Sarah Moorman. "THE INFLUENCE OF THE SOCIAL NETWORK ON MARRIED AND UNMARRIED OLDER ADULTS' MENTAL HEALTH." The Gerontologist Volume 56, no. Issue Suppl_3 (November 1, 2016): Page 513. https://doi.org/10.1093/geront/gnw162.2072.
14. Sackett-Fox, Kyrsten, Judith Gere, and John A. Updegraff. "Better Together: The Impact of Exercising with a Romantic Partner." Journal of Social and Personal Relationships 38, no. 11 (April 27, 2021): 3078–96. https://doi.org/10.1177/02654075211012086.
15. Sackett-Fox, Kyrsten, Judith Gere, and John A. Updegraff. "Better Together: The Impact of Exercising with a Romantic Partner." Journal of Social and Personal Relationships 38, no. 11 (April 27, 2021): 3078–96. https://doi.org/10.1177/02654075211012086.
16. Wilson, Chris M., and Andrew J. Oswald. "How Does Marriage Affect Physical and Psychological Health? A Survey of the Longitudinal Evidence." SSRN Electronic Journal, 2005. https://doi.org/10.2139/ssrn.735205.

17. Manzoli, Lamberto, Paolo Villari, Giovanni M Pirone, and Antonio Boccia. "Marital Status and Mortality in the Elderly: A Systematic Review and Meta-Analysis." Social Science & Medicine 64, no. 1 (January 2007): 77–94. https://doi.org/10.1016/j.socscimed.2006.08.031.
18. Holt-Lunstad, Julianne, Timothy B. Smith, and J. Bradley Layton. "Social Relationships and Mortality Risk: A Meta-Analytic Review." Edited by Carol Brayne. PLoS Medicine 7, no. 7 (July 27, 2010): e1000316. https://doi.org/10.1371/journal.pmed.1000316.
19. Brickel, M.A., LMFT, Robyn E. "Healthy Relationships Matter More Than We Think." PsychAlive, March 2, 2017. https://www.psychalive.org/healthy-relationships-matter/.
20. House, James S., Karl R. Landis, and Debra Umberson. "Social Relationships and Health." Science 241, no. 4865 (July 29, 1988): 540–45. https://doi.org/10.1126/science.3399889.
21. BYU News. "Happily Marrieds Have Lower Blood Pressure than Social Singles, BYU Study Shows," March 13, 2008.
https://news.byu.edu/news/happily-marrieds-have-lower-blood-pressure-social-singles-byu-study-shows.

22. Holt-Lunstad, Julianne, Wendy Birmingham, and Brandon Q. Jones. "Is There Something Unique about Marriage? The Relative Impact of Marital Status, Relationship Quality, and Network Social Support on Ambulatory Blood Pressure and Mental Health." Annals of Behavioral Medicine 35, no. 2 (March 18, 2008): 239–44. https://doi.org/10.1007/s12160-008-9018-y.
23. Petersen, Andrea. "Who Sleeps Better at Night?" WSJ, n.d. http://online.wsj.com/article/SB10001424052702303830204577446342515528860.html.
24. Aune, Krystyna S., and Norman C. H. Wong. "Antecedents and Consequences of Adult Play in Romantic Relationships." Personal Relationships 9, no. 3 (September 2002): 279–86. https://doi.org/10.1111/1475-6811.00019.
25. Rueckert, Carla L. Living the Law of One 101: The Choice, 2014.
26. tonyrobbins.com. "How to Innovate in Your Relationships | Tony Robbins," April 20, 2015. https://www.tonyrobbins.com/love-relationships/dont-get-stale/.
27. tonyrobbins.com. "6 Human Needs: Why Are They so Important?," April 5, 2021. https://www.tonyrobbins.com/mind-meaning/do-you-need-to-feel-significant/.

28. Gunn, Robin Jones. Coming Attractions. Katie Weldon Series #3, 2009.
29. Love Definition & Meaning | Britannica Dictionary. "Love Definition & Meaning | Britannica Dictionary," n.d. https://www.britannica.com/dictionary/love.
30. Affection Definition & Meaning | Britannica Dictionary. "Affection Definition & Meaning | Britannica Dictionary," n.d. https://www.britannica.com/dictionary/affection.
31. Intimacy Definition & Meaning | Britannica Dictionary. "Intimacy Definition & Meaning | Britannica Dictionary," n.d. https://www.britannica.com/dictionary/intimacy.
32. Passion Definition & Meaning | Britannica Dictionary. "Passion Definition & Meaning | Britannica Dictionary," n.d. https://www.britannica.com/dictionary/passion.
33. Khodaie, Laleh, and Omid Sadeghpoor. "Ginger From Ancient Times to the New Outlook." Jundishapur Journal of Natural Pharmaceutical Products 10, no. 1 (January 17, 2015). https://doi.org/10.17795/jjnpp-18402.

34. Tuarez, Jaimar. "What Part Of The Brain Controls Sexual Arousal? - NeuroTray." NeuroTray, January 28, 2021. https://neurotray.com/what-part-of-the-brain-controls-sexual-arousal/.
35. Commitment Definition & Meaning | Britannica Dictionary. "Commitment Definition & Meaning | Britannica Dictionary," n.d. https://www.britannica.com/dictionary/commitment.
36. Sexless Relationships: Causes, Effects & How To Fix It | mindbodygreen. "Sexless Relationships: Causes, Effects & How To Fix It | Mindbodygreen," n.d. https://www.mindbodygreen.com/articles/sexless-relationships-causes-and-how-to-fix.
37. lasvegasnevada.gov. "Getting Married In Las Vegas," December 29, 2021. https://www.lasvegasnevada.gov/News/Blog/Detail/getting-married-in-las-vegas.
38. Buergin, Miles. "Knowing Nevada: The Divorce Capital of the World." KRNV, n.d. https://mynews4.com/news/knowing-nevada/knowing-nevada-the-divorce-capital-of-the-world.
39. Grover, Shawn, and John F. Helliwell. "How's Life at Home? New Evidence on Marriage and the Set Point for Happiness." NBER, December 24, 2014. https://doi.org/10.3386/w20794.

40. MIT News Office, Anne Trafton. "Neuroscientists Reveal How the Brain Can Enhance Connections." MIT News | Massachusetts Institute of Technology, November 18, 2015. https://news.mit.edu/2015/brain-strengthen-connections-between-neurons-1118.
41. Lauer, Jeanette C., and Robert H. Lauer. The Play Solution: How to Put the Fun and Excitement Back into Your Relationship, 2002. https://doi.org/10.1036/0071390103.
42. Markman, Howard J., Scott M. Stanley, Susan L. Blumberg, Natalie H. Jenkins, and Carol Whiteley. 12 Hours to a Great Marriage: A Step-By-Step Guide for Making Love Last. Jossey-Bass, 2003. https://doi.org/10.1604/9780787968007.
43. Goldstein, E. Bruce. Cognitive Psychology Connecting Mind, Research, and Everyday Experience, 2014.
44. 16Personalities. "Free Personality Test | 16Personalities," n.d. http://www.16personalities.com/free-personality-test.
45. Inc., Gallup. "StrengthsFinder 2.0." Gallup.com, n.d. https://www.gallup.com/cliftonstrengths/en/254033/strengthsfinder.aspx.
46. Questionnaire Center | Authentic Happiness. "Questionnaire Center | Authentic Happiness," n.d. http://www.authentichappiness.sas.upenn.edu/testcenter.

47. The Peaceful Warrior's Way. "Life Purpose Calculator - The Peaceful Warrior's Way," n.d . https://www.peacefulwarrior.com/life-purpose-calculator/.
48. Truity. "The Enneagram Personality Test," February 15, 2023. https://www.truity.com/test/enneagram-personality-test.
49. Verywell Mind. "Here's Why Hugging Makes You Feel So Good," January 31, 2022. https://www.verywellmind.com/the-power-of-a-hug-on-your-health-5211361.
50. NLP World. "NLP Sensory Acuity | NLP Glossary," n.d. https://www.nlpworld.co.uk/nlp-glossary/s/sensory-acuity/.
51. Chapman, Gary. The Five Love Languages: The Secret to Love That Lasts, 2010.
52. The Love Language® Quiz. "The Love Language® Quiz," n.d. https://www.5lovelanguages.com/quizzes/love-language.
53. Passion Definition & Meaning | Britannica Dictionary. "Passion Definition & Meaning | Britannica Dictionary," n.d. https://www.britannica.com/dictionary/passion.
54. Science Of Being. "Law of Polarity | Science Of Being," n.d. https://www.scienceofbeing.com/the-law-of-polarity.

55. HeroRise. "What Defines Masculinity? Biology, Social Constructs, And Feminine Polarity," May 12, 2021. https://www.herorise.us/what-defines-masculinity-biology-social-constructs-and-feminine-polarity/.
56. Understanding Men & Women - AlisonArmstrong.com. "Understanding Men & Women - AlisonArmstrong.Com," n.d. https://www.alisonarmstrong.com/curriculum/und/umuw.html.
57. Gender in Chinese Philosophy | Internet Encyclopedia of Philosophy. "Gender in Chinese Philosophy | Internet Encyclopedia of Philosophy," n.d. https://iep.utm.edu/gender-in-chinese-philosophy/.
58. YouTube. "Men Are Experts on Femininity Because They Need It | Alison Armstrong," September 16, 2022, 17:50. https://www.youtube.com/watch?v=NySisSsKSSY.
59. Shella, Tamara A. "Art Therapy Improves Mood, and Reduces Pain and Anxiety When Offered at Bedside during Acute Hospital Treatment." The Arts in Psychotherapy 57 (February 2018): 59–64. https://doi.org/10.1016/j.aip.2017.10.003.

60. Understanding Men & Women - AlisonArmstrong.com. "Understanding Men & Women - AlisonArmstrong.Com," n.d. https://www.alisonarmstrong.com/curriculum/und/umuw.html.
61. Li, Qing. "Effect of Forest Bathing Trips on Human Immune Function." Environmental Health and Preventive Medicine 15, no. 1 (March 25, 2009): 9–17. https://doi.org/10.1007/s12199-008-0068-3.
62. Wen, Ye, Qi Yan, Yangliu Pan, Xinren Gu, and Yuanqiu Liu. "Medical Empirical Research on Forest Bathing (Shinrin-Yoku): A Systematic Review." Environmental Health and Preventive Medicine 24, no. 1 (December 2019). https://doi.org/10.1186/s12199-019-0822-8.
63. Antonelli, Michele, Grazia Barbieri, and Davide Donelli. "Effects of Forest Bathing (Shinrin-Yoku) on Levels of Cortisol as a Stress Biomarker: A Systematic Review and Meta-Analysis." International Journal of Biometeorology 63, no. 8 (April 18, 2019): 1117–34. https://doi.org/10.1007/s00484-019-01717-x.
64. Wen, Ye, Qi Yan, Yangliu Pan, Xinren Gu, and Yuanqiu Liu. "Medical Empirical Research on Forest Bathing (Shinrin-Yoku): A Systematic Review." Environmental Health and Preventive Medicine 24, no. 1 (December 2019). https://doi.org/10.1186/s12199-019-0822-8.

65. Wendel, Lizzie, and HealthyLine®. "Wellness Benefits of Negative Ions - HealthyLine®." HealthyLine®, May 17, 2017. https://healthyline.com/negative-ions-benefits/.

66. Perez, Vanessa, Dominik D Alexander, and William H Bailey. "Air Ions and Mood Outcomes: A Review and Meta-Analysis." BMC Psychiatry 13, no. 1 (January 15, 2013). https://doi.org/10.1186/1471-244x-13-2 9.

67. Biopsychology: Biological Rhythms - Infradian Rhythms | Psychology | tutor2u. "Biopsychology: Biological Rhythms - Infradian Rhythms," n.d . https://www.tutor2u.net/psychology/reference/bio psychology-infradian-rhythms.

68. Vitti, Alisa. "Infradian Rhythm: Your Guide to a Perfect Cycle - Flo Living." Flo Living, July 16, 2020. https://www.floliving.com/infradian-rhythm/.

69. Vitti, Alisa. "Infradian Rhythm: Your Guide to a Perfect Cycle - Flo Living." Flo Living, July 16, 2020. https://www.floliving.com/infradian-rhythm/.

70. PubMed. "The Lunar Cycle: Effects on Human and Animal Behavior and Physiology - PubMed," January 1, 2006. https://pubmed.ncbi.nlm.nih.gov/16407 788/.

71. Red Tent Goddess. "Red Tent Goddess | Sacred Feminine Sisterhood," n.d. https://www.redtentgoddess.com. https://bit.ly/RTG-CyclicalLiving.
72. Red Tent Goddess. "Red Tent Goddess | Sacred Feminine Sisterhood," n.d. https://www.redtentgoddess.com. https://bit.ly/RTG-CyclicalLiving.
73. Psychology Today. "14 Signs of Psychological and Emotional Manipulation," January 1, 2023. https://www.psychologytoday.com/us/blog/communication-success/201510/14-signs-psychological-and-emotional-manipulation.
74. Understanding Men & Women - AlisonArmstrong.com. "Understanding Men & Women - AlisonArmstrong.Com," n.d. https://www.alisonarmstrong.com/curriculum/und/umuw.html.
75. Deida, David. The Way of the Superior Man: A Spiritual Guide to Mastering the Challenges of Women, Work, and Sexual Desire (20th Anniversary Edition), 2017.
76. Safe space Definition & Meaning - Merriam-Webster. "Definition of SAFE SPACE," March 3, 2023. https://www.merriam-webster.com/dictionary/safe+space.

77. Kiecolt-Glaser, Janice K., Timothy J. Loving, Jeffrey R. Stowell, William B. Malarkey, Stanley Lemeshow, Stephanie L. Dickinson, and Ronald Glaser. "Hostile Marital Interactions, Proinflammatory Cytokine Production, and Wound Healing." Hostile Marital Interactions, Proinflammatory Cytokine Production, and Wound Healing | Wound Care, Infection, Healing | JAMA Psychiatry | JAMA Network, December 1, 2005. https://doi.org/10.1001/archpsyc.62.12.1377.
78. Rosenberg, Marshall B. Nonviolent Communication: A Language of Life. Nonviolent Communication Guides, 2015.
79. Request Definition & Meaning | Britannica Dictionary. "Request Definition & Meaning | Britannica Dictionary," n.d. https://www.britannica.com/dictionary/request.
80. Demand Definition & Meaning | Britannica Dictionary. "Demand Definition & Meaning | Britannica Dictionary," n.d. https://www.britannica.com/dictionary/demand.
81. Quote by Marianne Williamson: "The way of the miracle-worker is to see all hum..." "A Quote by Marianne Williamson," n.d. https://www.goodreads.com/quotes/459068-the-way-of-the-miracle-worker-is-to-see-all-human.

82. Avery, Lee S. "NLP Techniques - Pattern Interrupt or State Break." EzineArticles, January 9, 2014. https://ezinearticles.com/?NLP-Techniques---Pattern-Interrupt-or-State-Break&id=8238998.
83. Lehnardt, Senior Writer Karin. "59 Interesting Facts about Joseph Stalin | FactRetriever." 59 Terrifying Facts about Joseph Stalin | FactRetriever, August 31, 2017. https://www.factretriever.com/joseph-stalin-facts.
84. A Course In Miracles. "A Course In Miracles – Complete Searchable Online Web Edition of ACIM," n.d. https://acim.org/acim/en.
85. A Course In Miracles. "A Course In Miracles – Complete Searchable Online Web Edition of ACIM," n.d. https://acim.org/acim/en.
86. Ferriss, Tim. "Why You Should Define Your Fears Instead of Your Goals." Tim Ferriss: Why you should define your fears instead of your goals | TED Talk, n.d. https://www.ted.com/talks/tim_ferriss_why_you_should_define_your_fears_instead_of_your_goals.
87. Positive, The Daily. "Top 10 Regrets Of The Dying." The Daily Positive, July 18, 2014. https://www.thedailypositive.com/top-10-regrets-dying/.
88. BBC News. "Doctor Shares Dying Children's Wishes: 'Be Kind and Eat Ice Cream,'" n.d. https://www.bbc.com/news/health-42909326.

89. Positive, The Daily. "Top 10 Regrets Of The Dying." The Daily Positive, July 18, 2014. https://www.thedailypositive.com/top-10-regrets-dying/.

About The Authors

Jaslin and Yusuf Varzideh, a married couple from Florida, have been living their dream of traveling the world together since March 2020. They keep their relationship strong by going to workshops and reading countless books on communication, love, relationships, and more.

They were both natural writers and entrepreneurs much of their lives. They have both built businesses and began writing early in life and then started blogs, book clubs, did freelance work, and created a publishing company. When not writing, they read, learn something new, hike to rivers, or cuddle with their teddy bears, Chance and Destiny. Their mission in life is to spread love and encourage others to love one another unconditionally.

Printed in Great Britain
by Amazon

24362840R00119